I0449118

Heal Your Memories, Change Your Life

Move on in Your Life to a Phenomenal Present and Future

FRANK HEALY,
the Memory Healer

BALBOA.
PRESS
A DIVISION OF HAY HOUSE

Copyright © 2013 Frank Healy.
Interior Graphics/Art Credit: Jeanette Baker

All rights reserved. No part of this book may be used or reproduced
by any means, graphic, electronic, or mechanical, including
photocopying, recording, taping or by any information storage retrieval
system without the written permission of the publisher except in the
case of brief quotations embodied in critical articles and reviews.

Balboa Press books may be ordered through booksellers or by contacting:

Balboa Press
A Division of Hay House
1663 Liberty Drive
Bloomington, IN 47403
www.balboapress.com
1-(877) 407-4847

Because of the dynamic nature of the Internet, any web addresses or
links contained in this book may have changed since publication and
may no longer be valid. The views expressed in this work are solely those
of the author and do not necessarily reflect the views of the publisher,
and the publisher hereby disclaims any responsibility for them.

The author of this book does not dispense medical advice or
prescribe the use of any technique as a form of treatment for physical,
emotional, or medical problems without the advice of a physician,
either directly or indirectly. The intent of the author is only to offer
information of a general nature to help you in your quest for emotional
and spiritual well-being. In the event you use any of the information
in this book for yourself, which is your constitutional right, the author
and the publisher assume no responsibility for your actions.

Any people depicted in stock imagery provided by Thinkstock are
models, and such images are being used for illustrative purposes only.
Certain stock imagery © Thinkstock.

Printed in the United States of America.

ISBN: 978-1-4525-7967-2 (sc)
ISBN: 978-1-4525-7969-6 (hc)
ISBN: 978-1-4525-7968-9 (e)

Library of Congress Control Number: 2013914259

Balboa Press rev. date: 08/15/2013

To my wife Janet, we have many great memories and are building more with each passing day, month and year

Table of Contents

Preface

You have an amazing memory. The key to realizing that amazing memory can be found in unlocking your brain's potential and clearing the cobwebs. The road down memory lane can be hazy and blurred, but there are ways to clear the haze and see your past as if it happened just yesterday.

Try to recall a memory of which you only have a vague recollection. Ask yourself the following questions.

- **Where was it?**
- **Who was there?**
- **What do I remember seeing?**
- **What do I remember hearing or smelling?**
- **How do I feel about the events that occurred?**

Chances are that by taking some uninterrupted time and answering these questions, you will recall the event more vividly.

Reading *Heal Your Memories, Change Your Life* will take you through a variety of techniques to retrieve your memories and to learn from them. As a Licensed Professional Counselor, I have used these techniques to help hundreds of clients through the years.

Having a good memory can benefit you in many ways. After diligently working through the exercises presented in this book, you will know how to recall past memories in detail in order to turn any negative emotions associated with those past memories into positive emotions, and also how to extract valuable lessons from those memories to help propel you forward in many areas of your life. A good memory can enable you to stay organized and in control of your life.

You can also be in control of your life by making a conscious effort to control your thoughts. Everyone has moments when they do not have to be thinking about anything, such as when they are sitting around watching television, eating dinner, bathing or showering, gardening, or doing housework. Many people use that time to visualize their goals, to daydream, or to think through any issues they may be facing. It is true that if you do not make an effort to control your thoughts, your mind will tend to gravitate towards personal problems. You can instead dwell on positive memories from your past. Whether it's a vacation you took five years ago that you especially enjoyed, a special time with family or friends, or a personal accomplishment which you were particularly proud of, reliving positive events from your past is enjoyable.

Each of us would like to consider ourselves happy and successful. We want our interpersonal relationships to work well, we want job satisfaction, and we want to keep anxiety and depression at bay. In recent years, the field of psychology has taken a positive spin. Therapy is no longer only about curing depression, anxiety, or addictions. Therapy now also includes learning techniques to use your mind to achieve your goals, achieve satisfaction in your life, and to improve the overall quality of your life. *Heal Your Memories, Change Your Life* will help you improve the quality of your life by teaching you to take control of your thoughts, memories, and emotions.

Introduction
by Dr. Yvonne Kaye

(Author of The Child That Never Was and
Credit, Cash, and Codependency)

I am not sure whether this is an introduction or a gratitude list. Frank Healy most definitely needs to change his name to Frank Healer—without doubt. I write that sincerely as I have struggled with past trauma for many years, sought treatment, progressed well. However, when I read this amazing book I realized there are still steps to grow and change. In addition to living with trauma, I was a fine actress—nobody knew. Presenting at prestigious conferences, one would never think that once I walked off that stage, the woman I knew was insecure and questioning . . . Most people are able to hide and become part of their own secrets as being controlled by the past is a nightmare of huge proportions.

The title says it all—memories can make or break us. When reading the manuscript I was reminded of my personal Mentor, Dr. Viktor Frankl who wrote in his masterpiece, Man's Search for Meaning ". PEOPLE MAKE CONSCIOUS DECISIONS ON THE WAY THEY FEEL". He wrote that in Auswitchz Concentration Camp in the 1940s. On reading it in 1968 I thought—if he can say that in his environment, surely

I can make decisions out in the free world. It isn't often that I put any writer in the category of Dr. Frankl. I do now—Frank Healy. Quite extraordinary—Frankl and Frank! Frank has taken that philosophy to a level of magnificent simplicity, proving that people can change their lives and instructs how to do so, thought process by thought process.

I knew Frank many years ago, He writes about that time. I recall him demonstrating his astonishing ability in memorizing dates, days, and years. It was at that time I discovered there was far more to his genius—yes, genius—than remembering which day was on the given date and invited him to teach a course which was very successful. Since that time, 22 years ago, he has developed his expertise, counseling, teaching, writing about what amounts to different aspects of Post-Traumatic Stress Disorder. It is a vast subject as people have been emotionally paralyzed for most of their lives due to memories of childhood fears, abusive situations like bullying, incest, rape, There are many more incidents cited in this remarkable book.

HEAL YOUR MEMORIES, CHANGE YOU LIFE is not book of statistics. It is a book of life, of hope, and of self-worth. The reality of those who made unhealthy choices in life due to past pain and grief and continue to do so is expressed with compassion and caring. The difference in feeling sorrow for those afflicted and actually doing something to change it, is right here, beautifully written and explicit with simple steps. It is a work of art.

CHAPTER 1

Healing Outside Memories Is an Inside Job

He remembered everything, the good times, the tough times, the beautiful, the ugly. You name it, he remembered

it. It began when he was five years old. Home from school and too sick to be up playing with toys, he lay in bed and looked at the calendar. By the end of the week, he had memorized the entire year of 1966. As the years went by, each day he would make mental notes of which day it was when this or that event happened.

Sometimes it was fun to remember everything. He could look back at his childhood and remember happy times on the beach with his family and friends, swimming in the ocean, boating in the bay, going to the boardwalk, the bursts of hysterical laughter while enjoying Thanksgiving dinner with his grandparents. He remembered every family picnic, and he remembered every Christmas morning, including which presents he did or didn't get each year.

His birthday memories included who came to the party, at what restaurant the family dined, the palatial delights that were indulged. He also remembered the carnival across the street which always happened to be the same week as his birthday.

Then there were the good times in school. He had various roles in the school plays, including Beelzebub in *Saint George and the Dragon* and the young boy in *A Christmas Carol* who Scrooge sends to buy the turkey. Never mind that he stood a head taller than the boy who played Scrooge. There were the two game saving catches in Little League, and the award he won for being the best English student at his junior high graduation. He was even elected president of his sixth grade class.

He remembered all the good times with friends. Canoeing on the river, crawling through manholes and being relieved that he and his friend lived. Playing arcade games at the shore. Pulling pranks at fraternity parties such as trashing someone's room while they were indisposed in another. He not only remembered his first kiss, but his second, third, and every kiss thereafter. What a great life to remember!

Having a great memory could be a pain in the brain at other times. How would you like to remember every nasty thing that every kid in school ever said to you or did to you? Would you like to remember every time your boss yelled at you at a job?

There were those kisses, but there were also painful breakups. There were times of being recognized for good job performance, but there was also the time of being permanently laid off from his first job after college. They had the nerve to say, "You can either hate us or be thankful for the experience." Unbelievable!

He also had a plethora of mixed memories, including a tour of Europe and a tour of American Battlefields. The sights were great, but the company left much to be desired.

There were mixed moments in school, too. He remembered playing the trumpet in the school show *Guys and Dolls*. When he auditioned with his trumpet, the band director bluntly stated, "You sound good, I'm surprised."

As the years went by, the memories grew and would randomly flash into his consciousness. He not only recalled

the sights and sounds, but his nerves would flood with intense feelings as if he were experiencing the memory at that very moment. One moment to the next would bring a roller coaster of intense laughter, mourning, or anxiety depending on which memory popped into the forefront of his brain.

Then one day, he had a life-changing thought. What if he could find a way to hold onto the good feelings from the good memories while at the same time, reduce or eliminate the occurrence and intensity of the bad memories and the roller coaster of emotions that those bad memories brought with them? Being a good student, and an imaginative soul, he decided to experiment with his mind. His brain would be the laboratory, and the memories would be the research subjects.

Day after day, he performed different experiments with his happy and unhappy memories. This was quite a feat for a teenager. However, since he memorized an entire year of the calendar at age five, maybe mental gymnastics with his memories was not the stretch that it seemed.

Besides being imaginative, the young man was also an astute observer of human nature. He noticed that while other people did not remember as many events as he did, people were affected by their memories. Kids who were bullied at school either became shy or they became bullies themselves. People whose spouses died seemed to never be happy again. He would often notice that many people would mope and sulk if they had lost a lover or did not get a job they wanted.

These observations of human nature made him angry and compassionate. He felt angry because it seemed unfair that anyone should be stuck in the past as a victim of their unpleasant memories. He felt compassionate because he wanted to help people. Between the fascination with memory and the emotions elicited by studying human nature, it seemed only fitting that he should study psychology in college.

You may have surmised by now that this man is me. **I have dedicated my life to controlling my own mind as I have so many memories in it, and I live to help people do the same through my counseling and coaching work.**

The methods that I have discovered and learned have enabled me to help hundreds of people recover more of their good memories, and to use their bad and negative memories as positive learning experiences. This book will help you achieve the same happiness, contentment, and success that my clients have achieved.

For me, having hyperthymesia, the ability to remember every day of one's life with near perfect detail, is a gift. First, it is a gift because there have only been, at the time of this writing, thirty-two other documented cases of people with the same ability. Second, it is a gift because it brings with it the ability to recall many positive memories instantly, and the ability to learn lessons from the memories that seemed negative.

Everyone has a plethora of memories that they do not recall, but with the right encouragement and the right tools, those lost memories can be retrieved. The main reason people forget information and episodes in their lives is that they are busy with everyday life. They have stress and anxiety, both of which temporarily inhibit memory. They may also just think that they can't remember because they believe that they can't. Other people suppress their memories due to trauma in their lives. They prefer not to remember.

Many people suppress memories. Perhaps you do too and are reading this book because you want to remember more. However, you may wonder: what are the benefits of retrieving painful memories? Would it not be better to leave them alone and go about your business?

Some people seem to be able to just move on, forget the past, and be happy. I have had people who were not my counseling clients say things such as, "My father yelled at me all the time when I was growing up, but it doesn't matter." "My first boyfriend was abusive, but now I am in a great relationship." These people may or may not have been able to put the past behind them. Some of them may be in denial. This means that they are not aware of how they are affected by the memory.

Others may genuinely have let go and may mean it when they say, "It doesn't matter." Hardy personality is a characteristic we ascribe to people who are uncommonly resilient and can bounce back from anything.

I knew a woman who had a cancer operation when she was just twenty-seven years old. When she awoke from the surgery, she said, "May I go home and make dinner now?" Some people just seem to naturally let go, put things behind them, and quickly move on.

If everyone had a hardy personality, therapists would either be unemployed or doing something else. I would probably be a historian or an archivist. Maybe I would be tending a graveyard and keeping death and burial records. However, since people need help, there is an extensive field of counseling. Most of us do not bounce back as quickly as the hardy ones. When something traumatic happens, the effects stay with us unless we deal with them.

It is important to understand how our memories stick with us and affect our every day behavior. Frequently in my practice, I have clients who have self-defeating patterns for example. Some clients seem to reach success but then sabotage it. They fare well on a job interview but at the end, they may say something that disqualifies them.

During my college years, I worked in a museum for ethnic studies. A well-qualified candidate came in for a job interview and the museum staff seemed excited about having her. Despite the initial excitement, this woman ruined her chances before the interview ended. She asked the librarian, "Can you trace your genetics?" I do not know if she meant to say "Can you trace your genealogy?" rather than what she actually said, or if she was indeed ignorant of the difference between the two terms. However, this one error cost her chance at the job.

I also knew a young man in college who professed that he really wanted a girlfriend. However, when he talked to women, he would start well but inevitably he would say something which caused the ladies to not have any interest in him. He might have made a rude remark about her appearance or talked about someone who he knew she did not like. Consequently, he repeatedly sabotaged his chances. Other people start well in a new job and unwittingly stop producing. Then there are the millions of people who start a diet, lose some weight and then gain it back. I know this has never happened to you!

People need to understand why they self-sabotage. When I counsel people, I ask them if they believe they deserve to have a good job, or whether or not they deserve to be in a good relationship. If they believe they do not deserve good things, then I will work with them to change their beliefs. However, some clients do believe that they deserve good things but are unsure of why they ruin their own success. For these clients, it helps to uncover traumatic memories where they may have developed self-defeating beliefs that now affect their lives.

For example, If someone was always told that they don't deserve anything good, or that their parents' divorce was their fault, they will believe that they are bad and don't deserve success or happiness. Therapy then consists of the cognitive technique of changing erroneous and negative beliefs adopted at the time of the traumatic incident into healthier ones.

Marriage is another important area of life where past hurts and negative beliefs are usually hiding. A common source of contention within a marriage is accusations containing the words "always," "never," "inevitably," "typically," and other such absolute terms. During marital therapy, I often am able to coach a couple into recalling a time when the accusation they are referring to didn't actually happen, leading to less judgment and more satisfaction for both parties. For example, suppose the husband accuses his wife by saying, "You always override anything that I suggest we do with the house." Usually, a generalized statement like this comes when only one incident has occurred. Maybe the husband has just suggested they build a new deck, to which she responded that they don't have the money. He follows up with the statement that she always overrides him. Then I ask both of them to recall a time that he made a suggestion and she agreed with him. She then recalls that last year, he suggested they paint the house. They looked at samples and agreed on a color scheme for each room, and then they painted. By her recalling a memory that refutes the "never" belief, he then is able to see that his wife is not as controlling as he thought.

Recalling your memories can help you with different issues you might be experiencing in your life. For example, maybe you have an issue with your boss at work. You get knots in your stomach every time he asks to speak with you about something. To try to understand why you have this issue with your boss, it may be helpful to remember your experiences with parents, teachers, former bosses, and other authority figures. Maybe your parents were overly critical and you are projecting the fear of criticism into the relationship you have now with your boss.

Suppose you have a problem sticking to an exercise program. You might uncover that you were the last one picked for teams in gym class, so now you have a generally negative attitude towards exercise. Maybe you eat too many comfort foods, such as pizza, cheesecake, or ice cream. Then you uncover from your past that you had a lack of emotional support in your life. Maybe you have thought about going back to college for your doctoral degree but can't seem to push yourself to do it. You might uncover memories of how your parents discouraged you from pursuing higher education. "It's just not what we do in our family," or "You could have a nicer car if you didn't waste money on college."

You might be wondering why you would ever want to remember these negative things. Memories like these would only make you sad, angry, or less self-confident. The problem is that even if you do not recall the memories, the effects of those memories will still remain with you. You may be stuck in a pattern of bad relationships, failures at jobs, or low self-esteem because of those memories and the emotions and beliefs tied to them. However, as you do the exercises in this book, keep the following ideas in mind:

- **As you are instructed to recall unpleasant memories, try to think of them as learning experiences.**
- **As painful or uncomfortable as some of your memories may be, you will be taught how to eliminate the disabling and negative feelings associated with those memories.**
- **You will learn to extract and retain lessons from bad memories and you will learn how you can apply those lessons to your life now.**

When you recall an unpleasant memory, you may blame yourself for letting it happen, you may think that it happened because there is something wrong with you, or you may be tempted to think that the other people involved were mean people for what they did to you. All three of these interpretations can and will produce anger, anxiety, sadness, or low self-esteem.

Let's look at a hypothetical example. Suppose you recall a time when you ran into some bullies after school and they beat you up. First, you may blame yourself for letting it happen. You may think that perhaps you should have carried a knife to school, or maybe you should have made sure that you were accompanied by other people while you were walking around. Maybe you think that something is wrong with you or that you are just the kind of person who others see as weak. You may say to yourself, "I hope all those Neanderthals die, go to jail, or wind up with a painful and terminal disease." None of these thoughts however will bring you happiness or contentment.

Imagine turning an experience like this one into a lesson. You could think back and recall how you used to walk in the hallways at school looking like a scared rabbit after being abused by your schoolmates. Now you realize that you still sometimes walk and talk like you have no self-confidence or any sense of safety. A memory like this can be a life lesson.

There are ways to eliminate the bad feelings associated with a memory. As you read through this book and do the exercises, you will learn techniques for eliminating the bad feelings. You will also learn life lessons and eliminate anger or low self-esteem.

You will also learn to use the techniques in this book to recall pleasant and good memories from your past. Psychology has shown that the more you experience certain thoughts and feelings, the easier it is to later recall and access those thoughts and feelings in your mind. Therefore, if you spend a lot of time recalling good memories, you will find it easier to retrieve the pleasant feelings you had and experience them again now.

For example, think of a song that reminds you of a good time that you had in the past. When you hear the song on the radio or on your iPod or MP3 player, you feel the same feelings in the present moment as if you were having the experience from the past right now. You can have the same experience when you recall the details of a pleasant memory, and as you more frequently recall pleasant memories, the more time you will spend feeling good.

Perhaps in your effort to recall pleasant memories however, you find that so many of your memories are rather unpleasant. You might think that you are one of those people who nothing good ever happens to. Maybe so many things don't go your way and you are starting to see a never ending pattern of defeat.

For example, perhaps you had a fight with a friend and now you think, I am such a good person, why are people always fighting with me? Then you encounter someone you knew in school who was two grades behind you but is now making twice your income. You think to yourself, nothing ever goes right with me at work either. I will never get ahead. All of these negative thought patterns leave you feeling stressed and tired allowing your body to succumb to illness and then you think to yourself, I don't even have good health anymore.

When you let the negative attitudes and thoughts take over, you block memories of good things that have happened to you and you perpetuate a downward spiral of self pity. However, if you make a concentrated effort to recall good things that have happened, you will stop feeling like a victim. It has been my experience that if you get anyone to recall enough of their memories, they will discover that they have a plethora of good and bad memories. People are no different in that respect.

If you do the exercises in this book and still find that you are recalling more bad memories than good, it may help to spend more time dwelling on the positives. Even if your unhappy memories outweigh your happy memories in number, you can focus to expand the good feelings from the good memories. You can overcome the perception of victimhood and feel good about yourself and your life.

Sometimes, you might only be able to recall some of your memories in a more general way. Perhaps you remember an event, but not many of the details. You may recall that your last vacation was to Europe or to the beach. Maybe you remember a date or a night out with a group of friends but anything other than where you went and who was there is gone. Being able to recall more of the details of a vacation or a date usually will make the memory more fun and rewarding.

Wouldn't it be nice if you not only recalled a European vacation, but also everything that you saw, most or all of the people you met, what souvenirs you bought, conversations with the people around you, the food, and the good times on the road travelling from country to country? Or, if you remember a night out with friends, wouldn't it make for a more enjoyable memory if you could recall how you joked around and laughed together, who you met when you got there, and the show you saw together? Exercise 1A will give you tools you can use to recall more details of memories.

Exercise 1A—I Remember More Than I Thought I Did

You will need a pen and paper, or a blank Word document on your computer. I recommend you buy a hardbound journal or notebook where you can keep all of your notes from all of the exercises to come. By doing this, you will be able to review your notebook from time to time to see how you have progressed and what you have achieved. If you will be using a Word document, save the file for later use and review.

1. Pick a recent memory. It could be a party, a day at the beach, buying a new pet, or a day with your children or grandchildren. It can be any memory that makes you feel good when you remember it.

2. Take about five minutes and record everything that you can recall about that memory. Don't be overly rigid about timing. The purpose here is to have fun and recall a pleasant memory. Take your time with this step and recall as many details as you can naturally.

3. After finishing Step 2, take another few moments to answer the following questions about your memory.

   • Where were you? If the memory includes multiple locations, include all of them.

   • Who were you with? If you are recalling a memory where you were in multiple locations over a course of time, the people may have been the same or different during that time period.

   • What interactions did you have? Maybe you recall joking with a friend, or you may recall a kiss if it was a date.

   • What things did you see? Close your eyes and try to visualize the environment from your memory. If you were at a play or an opera for example, you may recall the stage décor and the layout of the theater.

   • What do you remember hearing? If you were at a concert, you will recall the music and the cheering. If you were getting a massage, you might recall the soft background music.

- **What were you feeling? If it was a day at the beach, you may recall the hot sand on your feet and the feel of riding waves.**
- **Were there any memorable smells or scents? The sense of smell stimulates more memories than any other.**
- **Was there food involved? Never forget those tacos in Mexico or crab cakes in Maryland.**

After going through the questions in Step 3, do you recall more details about the memory than you did after finishing Step 2?

Congratulations, you have just completed Exercise 1! If you recall more now than you did when you started the exercise, you have just proven that you can easily recall details of a memory by simply answering a few questions, and you did it all without the aid of pictures, talking to others who were there, or smelling anything. It is also possible that when you were doing Step 3 of the exercise, similar memories to the one you picked may have surfaced. For example, if you picked a memory of a vacation, recalling that vacation may have sparked memories of other vacations. If you remembered a particularly enjoyable Thanksgiving dinner, it is likely that memories of other family dinners also came to mind. Using sights, sounds, feelings, scents, and tastes can trigger many memories, and make the memory you are recalling more vivid.

What if you were not able to answer the questions in Step 3? There could be several reasons for this. Maybe you recalled a lot just by writing the paragraph as instructed in Step 2. Maybe the memory itself just didn't have a lot of details to be remembered. Maybe you recalled sounds and feelings but not many sights. Don't get discouraged if you couldn't answer all or any of the questions. As we go through the chapters of this book, we will do many exercises. If this one did not help you, hang in there. The same exercise may not help every person, but there are many things we can try that will help you!

As you recalled the sights, sounds, feelings, smells, and tastes in Step 3, did you remember anything negative even though you were focusing on a positive memory? Most times when you recall a good memory, bad memories or feelings will also surface. Maybe you remember playing basketball and winning the game. However, after your win, you might also remember that you tripped over your own feet on the way back to the locker room and people laughed at you.

Most people recall events with mixed feelings. However, if the positives outweigh the negatives, then you will feel positive about the event as a whole. In a later chapter, we will do an exercise which involves overcoming bad feelings by using good feelings.

I recall every day of my life since I was six years old, good and bad. People frequently ask me if it is a burden to remember everything. I tell them that I have learned to look at the not so pleasant memories as life lessons, and I have used the techniques that you are going to learn in this book to eliminate the negative feelings from past memories.

Essentially, I remember at least one event from every day since 1966. Many of the events I remember carry with them the same emotional intensity as if they were occurring in the present moment. Naturally, it is nice to remember trips to the beach, parties, good times with family and friends, and all the happy moments.

The dark side of my ability is that I would remember upsetting experiences including deaths in the family, romantic breakups, slights from others, illnesses, and all other manner of life's travesties with the same emotional intensity as if they were happening right now. I have learned to release the negative feelings and retain the positive feelings by using the techniques you will learn in this book.

When you remember events as intensely as I do, you discover that there are usually positive and negative aspects of any event in your life. Often you recall the experience with mixed feelings. If someone asked you about the event you might say it was okay or perhaps just all right.

Recently, or to be specific, on Saturday, August 25, 2012 my sister and her family had come to visit my wife and I for the weekend. We went to the beach at Stone Harbor, New Jersey, where my mother-in-law lives on the bay front. We packed our things and got ready to go to the beach. On the walk down, we joked around and teased each other.

When we arrived at the beach, I jumped in the water with my grandchildren, my niece, and my nephew. My niece navigated the rough waves with incredible bravery. I demonstrated body surfing to my nephew and my grandson. I am well qualified since I have been riding waves since Sunday, July 14, 1974.

On one ride, I rode in so far that my face scraped the sand. A minute later, my grandson told me that my nose was bleeding. I asked the lifeguard for gauze and bandages and sat on the chair for a half hour until the bleeding stopped. Within another hour, I was swimming in the bay again as if nothing had happened.

You might look at an incident like that as trivial. After all, I lived and only needed to exercise minimal caution while riding waves over the next few days.

This incident might be comparable to the basketball game. Everything went well except for the trip while walking back to the locker room. Some people would look at the trip or the nosebleed and think that it should have ruined my whole day. Others might laugh about it a month later. Others might laugh about it immediately.

It is possible to neutralize negative feelings about an event in your life. In the next exercise we are going to take the memory that you used for Exercise 1A and learn to change any negative feelings you might have had.

Exercise 1B—Flooding the Negatives with Positives

You will need a pen and your journal, or your Word document from Exercise 1A.

1. **Think of the negative aspect of the memory recalled in Exercise 1A and write it on the top of a new page. Include the details of the incident, and the feelings.**

2. Give the feeling that you have when you recall the incident a rating on a scale of one to ten. One means you do not feel any negativity and ten means that you are totally anxious, depressed, or angry when you recall the memory.

3. Write at least five good things about the memory from Exercise 1A.

4. Close your eyes and imagine the memory. First, imagine the part that was not so good, even if that was the part that happened at the end. Spend only a few seconds imagining the negative part of the memory.

5. Now imagine the good things that you remember from the event. Spend at least a few minutes on this aspect of the memory, replaying the pleasant events in your head several times.

6. Now go back to imagining the unhappy part. Again only spend a few seconds imagining the negative.

7. Open your eyes. Now write on a scale of one to ten how thinking about the negative feels.

We will now evaluate how you fared on the exercise. It is probable that now you are feeling good about the experience, and the negative aspect does not matter to you.

If you scored a one on the scale in Step 7, then you have succeeded in flooding the negative feelings with positive feelings. If you scored two, three, or four, then you are probably a person who feels things very strongly. You still felt the negative feeling, but it was overpowered by the positive feelings. If you scored five or more on this activity, you may be someone who is habituated to feeling more unhappy than happy. Do you tend to dwell on negative events? When you think about the future, do you anticipate the worst?

You are not alone. Many people think of the worst possible thing that could happen in any given circumstance. Ironically, there is a reason you and others think negatively. Negative thoughts and thought patterns are a subconscious effort to avoid disappointment. If you anticipate the worst possible scenario and it actually happens, you will not be surprised or disappointed. On the other hand, if something good happens, you will be pleasantly surprised.

This might seem like good logic or common sense, however, there is a flaw to this logic. When you spend a large chunk of your day thinking negatively, you will experience the same sadness, aggravation, or anxiety as if the catastrophe is happening or has happened. If these negative expectations were replaced with positive expectations, you could be feeling happy and relaxed instead.

You may have unwittingly trained yourself to be unhappy. Keep in mind that this is not a blame game. The good news is that even though you may have unwittingly trained yourself to be unhappy, you can now wittingly condition and train yourself to be happy instead. The exercises in this book will teach you to be happier and more successful.

Exercise 1B, which you just completed was called "Flooding the Negatives with Positives" because you thought of the positive aspects of a memory and used them to flood and overpower the negatives aspects. Many of the exercises in the later chapters are similarly designed. You will be instructed to remember the positives with the negatives and make the positive feelings stronger. The positive feelings will overpower the negative feelings. This works for unhappy feelings even in real tragedies.

In this chapter you learned to:

1. **Recall details of your memories.**
2. **Take control of feelings associated with your memories.**

Your feelings and memories are also influenced by your beliefs. In the next chapter, you will learn how your beliefs were formed by memories, and how your beliefs in turn influence what you remember. We will also practice identifying beliefs formed from memories so that later, you can change negative beliefs and be happy and successful.

CHAPTER 2

How Your Memories Affect Your Beliefs

Yikes! My wife just asked me to put up a ceiling fan. I didn't know that was part of marriage! This was my first thought on Sunday, August 8, 2010 as I stood in my bedroom with a bunch of screws, nuts, bolts, and fan blades.

My head swirled with thoughts of how to get out of this. Certain beliefs emerged from the core of my mind. **I am a white collar worker. I don't know how to do mechanical stuff. Being a handy type guy isn't my forte. I have more patience with people and my clients than I do with things like ceiling fans.** However, these beliefs were contradicted by thoughts such as **I want to please my wife. I did spend the afternoon on the beach, so maybe now I should earn my keep. I do like a challenge.** Along with these thoughts came memories of the few other times in my life when I attempted to assemble things.

There was that cold night in a coworker's apartment, Monday, January 13, 2003. My friend and I were struggling to carry a large box containing a new treadmill into another friend's apartment. We clumsily carried the heavy box up the narrow apartment stairway with repeated pleas between the two of us to slow down, speed up, "Clockwise is that way!" Any spectators might have guessed that we were staging a comedy show or shooting a video for the television series *Funniest Home Videos*.

As we approached the first landing, my friend asked while panting, "Do you want to take a break?" Wanting to appear strong and as if I had some amount of stamina, I said, "No, let's keep going." My friend, still panting, replied, "Well, I need a break." I panted, sighed, and agreed. Finally, we got the treadmill up the stairs and into the apartment door. We still had all ten fingers and toes and had not dropped the box.

As we finally got the box into the apartment, I smelled spaghetti and meatballs. Our friend had made us a nice dinner as a reward for helping her with the treadmill. She asked if we would like to eat the spaghetti first, or assemble the treadmill first. Wisely, I voted for assembly first as we would probably not be very good at assembling after consuming pounds of spaghetti, tons of meatballs, and red wine to boot.

She brought us her tools and we proceeded to put the two sides together with ease. To my chagrin, my friend could not wait any longer to eat so we took a break. Much as I feared, he had three servings of spaghetti and drank three glasses of wine. I had half a glass and one serving. When we returned to work, he groaned and fell asleep.

Consequently, I finished the assembly. We turned on the machine and she tried it out. Mission accomplished!

As I returned to the present moment in my bedroom with a bunch of tools and fan parts, I sighed with the realization that that particular memory was not helping me to prove my case but rather showed that I was indeed capable of putting together the ceiling fan. My creative and determined mind fetched another memory. Sunday, March 5, 2006, a friend called and said she just got a new swing set and she was hoping that I could come over and help her put it together. It was one of those adult models. If Nat King Cole were still alive, he might do a song called "Swing Set Built For Two" as an addendum to "Bicycle Built For Two".

When we emptied the contents of the swing set box, I was overwhelmed by the plethora of nuts, bolts, and screws of all shapes and sizes. However, we then did what few people dare to do. We read the directions. With the assistance of the directions and a power drill, the work became routine. Two hours later, her backyard shone with a beautiful swing set.

So now I had no choice but to assemble and install the ceiling fan. My memories had proven that I can assemble things. My mouth said, "No problem, just leave me alone in here and I will have it fastened to the ceiling and working in no time." My brain however was thinking that I needed my wife out of the room so she wouldn't learn how many four letter words are in my vocabulary if I screwed this up.

At first, I dropped a couple of bolts and it was a pain getting down from the stepladder, crawling under the bed to retrieve them, and climbing back up the ladder. After that, it was all uphill and an hour later the room was decorated with a beautiful ceiling fan that provided a cool gentle wind deceptively similar to a tropical breeze.

Some people reading this book might remember a routine skit from *Saturday Night Live* in which the late Gilda Radnor would tell a bizarre story and conclude with the phrase, "Well it just goes to show," after which she would state some silly and off the wall conclusion. I will say that my ceiling fan experience was accidental proof that it just goes to show that you can accomplish new things if you believe you can. Sometimes you just need to search your memories, examine the beliefs that you have developed from those memories, and perhaps revise those beliefs if necessary. This chapter will teach you how to do just that!

Which comes first, the memory or the belief? The answer is both. Your brain will form and adopt beliefs based on your past memories. However, your beliefs will affect which memories you recall and which ones fade.

What exactly is a belief? First, let's explore what a belief is not. **A belief is not a fact.** We often treat beliefs as if they were facts.

For example, suppose you believe that all people who ride motorcycles are uneducated and unemployed street gang members. You meet someone at a party who has arrived on their motorcycle and they tell you about the doctoral program they are in and how they teach at a local college. Furthermore, they and their fellow weekend warriors raised more than ten thousand dollars to fund their church's mission program to Haiti. Suddenly, you need to change your belief about bikers.

No, beliefs are not facts. They are conclusions you have made about yourself, people, society, religion, and all other aspects of life. As seen from the previous example, when you get new information, you are forced to change your beliefs.

How do we make conclusions and form beliefs? Even from infancy, we are all detectives trying to make sense of life from what we experience. **If we were fed when we were hungry, if our diapers were changed when the pipes leaked, and if we were held and played with while growing up, we adopt the belief that the world is a safe place and people are good to us. However, if we do not get an immediate response when we cry to be fed, held, or changed, we adopt the belief that the world is scary and apathetic.**

In grade school, we formed beliefs about ourselves. If we are good in school, we form a belief that we are smart. If we are good in sports, we form a belief that we are athletic. **An athletic boy or a pretty girl will form the beliefs that they are popular and people like them.** Unfortunately, there are many kids who do not fall into any of these categories and **therefore form the belief that they are just average kids and will be average ordinary adults.**

Other beliefs are formed by the way adults treat us. **If adults make false promises, we form a belief that we can't trust people. If we were physically abused, we may form a belief that aggression is an effective way to get what we want. Someone in this situation will also more than likely form a belief that they are bad and vulnerable.**

When a child is physically or emotionally abused, their impulse can be to want to hurt and even physically destroy the abuser depending on how badly the abuser has hurt them. However, they know that they can't do that or they will not survive, particularly if the abuser is a parent. If they were to follow through with these impulses, the child would no longer have anyone to feed them or to provide them with a roof over their head. **Their alternative course of action then is to turn their anger in on themselves and form the belief that they are just no good. They may also believe that they deserved the abuse in some way, although they can't identify what they did.**

If you have memories of not finishing things that you have started, you might have a history of self-sabotaging. It may be that you formed negative beliefs about yourself through your earliest memories. Conversely, if you have achieved your goals, have a life that you are satisfied with, and are happy most of the time, than you have formed positive beliefs about yourself and your world.

You may recall from the last chapter that everyone has memories that elicit a feeling of joy when recalled. Everyone also has other memories that cause them to feel angry, sad, or anxious. It might seem logical to say that because we all have memories that carry the same emotional strings, we should all be the same in our emotional outlook on life. If logic prevailed, however, then why is it that some people are happy, successful, and confident, others are satisfied with some aspects of their lives, and still others are unhappy, miserable, sick, and fail at everything they undertake?

The answer is that while memories might trigger the same emotions from person to person, the beliefs formed from those memories and emotions will be different from person to person. Furthermore, beliefs formed years prior will determine which memories a person recalls now. For example, if you believe that you are smart, you could easily recall making the Dean's List in college and going on to finish doctoral work. You might even remember the details of the classes you took. However, there was also the day that you were sick in junior year and failed the final. It was one of your worst collegiate performances. You will probably not easily recall that memory because it is contradictory to your belief that you are smart.

Similarly, suppose you believe that you are athletic but not smart. Although you don't believe that you are smart, there was one time that you earned an A on a midterm and you were relieved because now your overall grade was high enough to allow you to keep playing football. Years later, you may remember that you played ball but forget that you ever got an A on a midterm.

What about the personal example I provided at the beginning of this chapter? I believed that I could not put together a ceiling fan, but then I recalled memories of successfully assembling a treadmill and a swing set. In that situation, I started with beliefs that I was not a handyman. However, there were other beliefs that made me determined to assemble that fan. These beliefs included:

- **I am a good husband, and putting this fan together is part of being a good husband.**
- **I always find a way to accomplish what I need to do.**
- **I like being successful.**
- **My wife will be happy when I am finished with this task.**
- **I will be doing more things around the house, so I might as well get used to handy man type work.**

With these beliefs pervading my brain, I was able to recall memories of similar situations, and then use those beliefs to successfully assemble the fan.

Changing your beliefs is not as hard as it may seem. In the following exercises, you will learn how to change your beliefs, and how to doctor your painful memories.

Exercise 2A—Beliefs to Adopt to Change Your Beliefs

Try for the rest of this chapter to adopt the beliefs listed below. Write them in your journal or record them in your Word document and read them to yourself until you really believe them. Say them out loud a few times.

- **My beliefs are not facts.**
- **My beliefs are conclusions I have drawn based on past memories.**

- **I created my beliefs to protect myself in the world as I saw fit.**
- **I choose beliefs that are useful to me.**
- **I can change my beliefs if different beliefs would serve me better.**
- **I do not need to keep any beliefs that cause me pain.**

If you had no trouble understanding and internalizing Exercise 2A, then you are well on your way to achieving the goal of healing your memories. However, if you were confused by the exercise, it may be that you feel that you don't have anything on which to base these beliefs. Most beliefs people have are based on past evidence.

Realistically, what if you have no evidence on which to base a new belief? If you have never been successful in anything you've done, how can you believe that you can be successful now? Hang in there, and I will show you how to develop beliefs that will build your confidence.

In Exercise 2B, you are going to pick a positive memory from your past and determine what good, helpful beliefs you derived from that memory. If that seems like an overwhelming task, I have included some examples here of possible memories that you could pick.

Example 1—Beliefs Adopted while Planting Spring Flowers and Vegetables with Dad

- I like spring.
- I like gardening.
- Playing in the dirt is fun.
- I feel special when I garden with dad.
- I enjoy physical activity.

You may notice that the first three beliefs are basic beliefs and are simply conclusions that you have drawn about the specific activity—gardening. General beliefs, however, are the kind of beliefs that you can apply to different areas of your life. I feel special could apply to everything that you do with your father throughout your life, not just gardening. The last belief could influence you to be the type of person who always exercises and stays in shape.

Example 2—Beliefs Adopted during a Dinner Conversation about Success and Careers

- Dinner is a good time to talk.
- Dinner is a good time to be with my family.
- My parents care about my siblings and I.
- I am proud of the accomplished adults in my family.
- I can be what I want to be if I work hard enough.

- **I am going to have a successful future.**
- **I can choose what I want to be.**

These are examples of positive beliefs. You also might derive some mixed beliefs from this experience.

- **Setting the table is boring and I hate it. If I work hard in school, I won't have a boring job for the rest of my life.**
- **My cousin is working as a courier for a paper company. I would rather be a doctor like my uncle.**
- **My sister is working as a cashier. I would rather be a lawyer like my aunt.**

Example 3—Beliefs Adopted while Playing on a Sports Team

- **I am great at basketball. I want to play professionally.**
- **If anything were to interfere with my desire to play professional basketball, I can be a coach or a gym teacher. Either way, it feels good to stay in shape.**
- **A lot can be accomplished by working as a team.**
- **I can feel good whether we win or lose, as long as I did my best.**

The last two bullets are general beliefs and can be applied to many aspects of life, such as your career and your marriage.

Hopefully you can see from these examples that identifying beliefs formed from memories is not difficult. All you have to do is think of the good feelings and benefits you gained from the memories. Studying these examples and doing the next exercise will assist you in deriving life lessons from unpleasant memories as well as pleasant ones. Let's now do an exercise where you review your own memories and find your beliefs.

Exercise 2B—Good Memory, Good Beliefs

You will need a pen and your journal, or your Word document.

1. **Pick a memory that was positive for you. Here are some suggestions to help you remember a specific memory:**

    - **An accomplishment you are proud of.**
    - **A time when you felt special or that someone cared for you.**
    - **A time when you felt connected to people.**
    - **A time when you learned a valuable lesson.**
    - **A regular event that you always anticipated with excitement.**

2. **Go back to Exercise 1A, Part 3. Answer all of the questions about the memory which you are using for**

this exercise. This includes the sights, sounds, feelings, and anything else that you can remember.

3. **Review what you have written and based on the feelings this memory elicits, write down what beliefs you may have adopted from this memory.**

What did you learn from Exercise 2B? You may have uncovered some beliefs that you did not know you had. Maybe you now understand why you have self-confidence and feel good about people, and maybe now you understand why you do something well.

But what if you had trouble identifying the beliefs you may have formed from the memory in Exercise 2B? Maybe you remembered everything you possibly could but still did not think of any beliefs. If you had this problem, do not get discouraged. Here is an exercise to help you identify beliefs formed from your memory.

Exercise 2C—Finding Your Beliefs

You will need a pen and your journal, or your Word document.

Take the memory you used in Exercise 2B and answer the following questions:

1. **Where did the memory take place?**
2. **How do you feel about that place or that occasion now?**

3. **Why do you feel that way?**
4. **Who did you interact with the most?**
5. **How do you feel about that person and people who are like them?**
6. **Why do you feel that way?**
7. **Did you accomplish something?**
8. **How do you feel about yourself based on that accomplishment?**
9. **Why do you feel that way?**
10. **Was there a pleasurable activity?**
11. **Is that activity still one of your favorite pastimes?**
12. **How do you feel when you do that activity now?**
13. **Why do you feel that way?**

I hope you took the time to do this exercise. If you had trouble with Exercise 2B, Exercise 2C will help to make sure that you are prepared to heal your memories in later exercises.

I realize it is tempting to read through a book and skip the exercises. You might have initially gotten a good feeling from hoping that there is something that you can do to enrich your life, but when it comes time to do the exercises, you don't want to put in the time for fear of failure or disappointment. What if it doesn't work? What if you can't do it and only other people can?

Well, if you don't try then you definitely will fail and it won't work. So don't be one of those people. Do the exercises and be successful!

Notice in Exercise 2C that questions one and two lead to three, questions four and five lead to six, questions seven and eight lead to nine, and questions ten, eleven, and twelve lead to thirteen. **The questions have been ordered this way to show you that when you recall a memory, and then you recall your feelings about that memory, you can then ask yourself why you felt that way in order to extract beliefs from the feelings.** You may have experienced this before if someone had asked you at some point why you were so happy for no apparent reason. Perhaps you would have responded, "Oh because it's finally the weekend and it's so beautiful outside." Or, someone could have asked you why were sad, to which you replied, "I am sad because my child is sick."

Usually you know why you feel a certain way so hopefully you will be able to answer questions three, six, nine, and thirteen. The answers to these questions are your beliefs.

By this time, you should have learned some positive beliefs you have about yourself, other people, the world, and activities that you enjoy. In the next chapter, you will explore how some events in your life have produced both negative and positive beliefs, and you will learn how to change the negative aspects of those experiences within your mind.

CHAPTER 3

Change Your Beliefs, Change Your Life

In the previous chapter, you learned how your experiences will lead you to form certain beliefs about yourself, other people, or the world. In the examples provided and the exercises that you completed, you were instructed to focus on positive and happy memories. Now we are going to take your learning further by recalling an event that you may have both positive and negative feelings about at the same time.

The material to follow will help you to realize that you can handle negative memories and find meaning in them. You will also see that you can change any disturbing beliefs that you have adopted. Lastly, and most importantly, you will learn that by changing your beliefs, you will also change the feelings that you have about the negative memories and you will no longer feel unhappy recalling those negative experiences.

As I mentioned in Chapter 1, I remember every episode in my life with such clarity that I even remember the date on which the events occurred. Sometimes this clarity is disadvantageous, but the following is an example from my life showing how I have used the methods in this book to turn a bad experience and its negative beliefs into something positive.

Thursday, November 13, 1975 was a gloomy, rainy day. I think we were getting the residue of the Lake Superior storm that three days earlier had caused the wreck of the *S.S. Edmund Fitzgerald*. I was due to have my trumpet test which would determine my grade in band. After I played the piece of music assigned to me in front of the band director, he said in a very matter of fact tone, "Your tone quality is not good. As a matter of fact, it stinks." He then offered to give me a B for the entire year if I would stop playing the trumpet and if I would take attendance each day. My career as a trumpeter seemed to go down with the ship.

About three years later, Thursday, February 16, 1978 was a cold night. A foot of snow glistened and shone in the moonlight. The blizzard of 1978 dumped more than fourteen inches of snow on the ground on February 5th, 6th, and 7th, then another couple of inches on the 13th and 14th. The winter wonderland seemed like it would be here forever as temperatures stayed below freezing for several weeks. Trees seemed to whistle a melody in the wind.

A week earlier, the choral director who was running the upcoming production of *Guys and Dolls* asked my class during a rehearsal if we knew a trumpeter to play in the mission band. I told him I still had my old trumpet so he asked me to audition.

I hadn't played my trumpet since that embarrassing event in 1975. When the choral director however asked me if I would audition for *Guys and Dolls*, I decided to suspend all the negative beliefs that I had formed about my ability to play and used the next few weeks to practice "Follow the Fold". When I auditioned, the music came out with unbelievable tone and rhythm. The choral director said it was good. The band director said, "It sounds good. I am surprised."

Negative beliefs acquired on November 13, 1975:

- **I am not a good musician.**
- **I will find other things to do and take that B for taking attendance.**

In the week leading up to February 16, 1978, I challenged the previous beliefs:

- **I can at least be good enough to play as a mission band member.**
- **I am good at singing and acting, so maybe I can do this.**
- **When I try, I will be satisfied that I did my best.**

Beliefs after February 16, 1978:

- **I have musical ability.**
- **It is nice to have this role in my last musical before graduation.**

By knowing how to change what I believe about any day of my life, I have acquired a general belief that every day is a good day. November 13, 1975 was a good day because it became an opportunity to reexamine my priorities and explore what I could do other then play the trumpet. Then February 16, 1978 became an opportunity to end my high school theater career on a good note, pardon the pun.

In the next exercise, you are going to pick a memory that you have both positive and negative feelings about. Here is an example with some suggestions.

Example 4—Mixed Reviews

- **You played sports in school. It was great when you won but when you lost, the coach yelled at you, and your father yelled at you if you got upset about losing.**
- **Your parents always praised you when you accomplished something, but they chastised you when you failed to meet their standards.**
- **You went on a nice vacation, but it was the end of a romance.**
- **You had a job that you liked but an annoying coworker.**

Let's look at the beliefs you might form based on these events.

From the first example with sports, the positive belief is that it is good to do your best and win. However, the negative belief is that you are only permitted to express positive feelings, and you are supposed to hold in your unhappy feelings. You may also develop a mortal fear of losing.

The second example is similar. Working hard and accomplishing something is great, but love and acceptance are based on merit. Often people who believe that they are only valuable when they achieve and produce are risks for suicide.

When you go on a nice vacation, you can develop an appreciation for the place you visited. Unfortunately the reverse is true—you might hate the place you visited because of the emotional association of hurt that you developed.

Imagine if you went to the Florida Keys. You always liked the sun, the blue water, the birds, the palm trees. However, your lover told you that they don't think the relationship is going to work, so now The Keys will be tainted with sadness. If this is the first time you went away and spent long periods of time with a lover, you could develop the belief that you can't have a relationship and get married, or that you are unattractive or impossible to live with. All of this happened because you liked to swim laps in the blue water and they wanted to spend the entire day lounging under the cabana guzzling Green Iguanas or Bahama Mama's.

Maybe you have a memory of a job that you liked. You liked the work, and you were friendly with your coworkers. However, there was this one coworker who always bothered you with nonsense when you were trying to get work done. Nobody liked this person and they clung to you thinking you were a nice person who would not tell them to get lost. They told you how nice you were, but to you it seemed insincere. They bent your ear about things you did not want to hear, such as announcing that they were going to the circus on Friday night. Come Monday, they bored you with every detail about the experience. What the clowns and elephants did, how the parking experience was, and who they were with when you don't know the people anyway. You bite your lip to prevent yourself from saying, "You are a big clown so why didn't you just join them?" Polite attempts to be excused from their presence met with manipulative comments such as, "Oh, you don't like me either." When you complained to a coworker, he just put on his tough voice and said, "He doesn't bother me because I would tell him where to go."

The positive beliefs from an experience like this might include:

- **I am glad I have a good job given that good jobs are hard to come by these days.**
- **I am glad I have a great boss and mostly good coworkers.**

Your negative beliefs may include:
- **I am a magnet for strange and annoying people.**
- **I am too nice so morons like him cling to me.**
- **I need to be more assertive like other people.**

Some of you reading this might be thinking, I don't want to uncover negative beliefs and memories, what's the point? Wouldn't it be better to remain blissfully unaware of this stuff? Ironically, it would not be better as you will not remove the negativity from your system if you don't identify that negativity first. In the next exercises, you will learn to take the negative beliefs and feelings out of a memory. Then you will be free of them!

Exercise 3A—Finding Your Mixed Beliefs

You will need a pen and your journal, or your Word document.

1. **Pick a memory that you have both positive and negative feelings about. Example 4 provided some suggestions.**
2. **Go back to Exercise 1A, Part 3 to help you describe the memory that you just selected in terms of sights, sounds, feelings, scents, and tastes.**
3. **Review what you have written and write the good and bad beliefs you adopted from this memory.**
4. **If you have trouble identifying your beliefs, review Exercise 2C and use it for this memory.**

Now that you have a combination of good and bad beliefs, you are going to turn the negative beliefs that you adopted into positive beliefs. This transformation will often occur by identifying life lessons within the experience being examined. Before we begin the next exercise, here are some examples of how you can change your beliefs.

When I work with my clients who are expressing thoughts and beliefs which produce anxiety, anger, or depression, I do a written exercise with them where they change their unhappy belief in small steps.

First, I write at the top of a sheet of paper what their unhappy belief is. Then I suggest a belief or thought that would be a slight improvement over the one that they expressed and I write it under the first belief.

Then I ask them if this belief feels better, worse, or the same as the first one. Usually the client says that the second one feels better, but sometimes they will say it feels the same. They almost never say that it feels worse.

You may be wondering why I don't go from a very negative belief to a positive one in one step. I have found from my twenty-four years of working in the counseling field that it is silly and even ridiculous to move too quickly.

Imagine if you were feeling depressed because you had a fight with your spouse or a friend. If you wrote on the top of the paper, **I am a lousy spouse/friend,** and then wrote underneath it, **I am the greatest person and everyone loves me,** you would not take the second statement seriously and your mind would be thinking a few choice words which are unprintable.

The only therapeutic value that you could glean from the above example is a good laugh. You would not feel any better about yourself and your friendship or relationship. It would be better to start with a thought that felt slightly better and more realistic. How about, **I am a good friend. We are just having a disagreement.** Then you could go to, **We can work this out. We have worked things out at other times. Maybe I should just take a time out and then arrange a time to talk later.** When you take several small steps like this rather than one giant leap, you are likely to feel better and eventually resolve the issue.

Let's review Example 4 and see how we can take small steps to change the unhappy and dysfunctional beliefs.

When you lost a game, the coach yelled at you, and your dad yelled at you if you got upset about the loss. The fact that your dad would yell at you has led you to form a belief that you must hold in and suppress your unhappy feelings. You can change that negative belief to:

- **When I am with trusted people, I can share my feelings.**
- **I am still okay if I am unhappy when we lose. It does not make me weak.**
- **I can accept that I am unhappy sometimes, but I don't have to stay grumpy.**
- **I can accept my grumpiness but then let it go.**
- **Accepting my feelings is important for my self-esteem.**

If your parents praised you when you performed well, but chastised you when you did not meet their standards, you might believe, **I am only lovable when I perform.** You could change that to:

- **I am okay the way I am.**
- **Everyone has bad days.**
- **I can please myself.**
- **I learn a lot when I make mistakes.**

If you lost your lover while on vacation, you might believe, **I can't have a relationship because I am unlovable.** You could change this belief to:

- **This was just one person's opinion.**
- **I still got a nice vacation out of the deal.**
- **The break up gave me freedom to be single and, later, to find someone else.**

Then there was the job with the annoying coworker. You believe, **I am a magnet for strange and annoying people. I am too nice so these weirdoes cling to me. I need to be more assertive like other people.** You could change the beliefs to:

- **This is a good lesson in assertiveness.**
- **It is flattering that people think that I am good to be with, but I can set reasonable limits too.**
- **I can take better care of myself by enforcing appropriate boundaries.**

By changing your beliefs about your memories, you change your feelings about them. It is possible, and even probable, that you have a memory that you don't like but it keeps invading your brain and your mood and you wish you could just forget it.

When you change the beliefs about a memory, it will knock the emotional charge out of it. Consequently, you will not keep dwelling on it, and then you will be free. Now let's try changing the beliefs you identified from the memory you used in Exercise3A.

Exercise 3B—Changing Your Feelings about Your Memory

You will need a pen and your journal, or your Word document.

1. **List all of the positive beliefs you have from Exercise 3A. This will remind you that there were positive aspects, and it will put you in a state of mind where you are thinking in a positive way.**
2. **Now at the top of the next page write a negative belief you have about the memory.**
3. **Starting underneath the negative belief, write a series of better feeling beliefs. Keep going down the page until you run out of ideas or are feeling better about the memory.**
4. **Read your list of better feeling memories a few times. Let yourself feel the feelings of the better beliefs. Keep reading it until you are feeling good.**
5. **Repeat Steps 2 through 4 with all of the negative beliefs you had for that memory.**

So what feelings do you have now for the memory you chose? If you feel mostly good feelings such as happiness and gratitude, then you have experienced your first healing of a memory. Congratulations! You are well on your way to healing all of your memories. If you don't feel any differently after this exercise, then try spending more time dwelling on your newly created beliefs.

Sometimes the changes that happen in our lives affect how we feel and what we think of a past memory. If you were fired from a job you liked but are now working at a better job, it will be easy to see the past firing as a good thing that happened to you. But if you were fired from a job and are still unemployed, you may have to be more creative to find meaning in being currently unemployed.

Perhaps you could think, **This is an opportunity to examine my priorities. I now have time to go fishing or hiking and to spend more time with the kids. I could learn all kinds of creative ways to save money.** The personal belief that I am expressing here is **there is always a way to reframe a memory in a positive way.**

Changing your beliefs about a memory is just one way to change how you feel about a past memory. Sometimes my clients do not immediately feel better about a past episode when they change their beliefs. They will tell me that they did not find many beliefs anyway. With this in mind, I created an additional exercise that can help you discover beliefs, and permanently change your feelings about an episode in your past.

In the '60s '70s and '80s, there was an unorthodox but popular type of therapy called psychodrama. Psychodrama was used in inpatient settings where there were many patients, because it takes a group of people to perform it successfully.

First, a patient was selected from the group by the psychodrama director to be the protagonist. The protagonist would sit in a chair and discuss a traumatic incident from their past. The director would sit in a chair facing them or they would call another client forward to act as the person who caused the trauma in the incident being discussed. It might be a critical parent, their boss, or kids who bullied them when they were younger.

Everyone acted the scene. Often the protagonist would be screaming hysterically or would let out an avalanche of tears as the feelings related to their trauma surfaced.

When the scene was completed, the director asked the protagonist how they wished things would have happened. For example, a man might have acted out yelling and abuse which was ongoing from his father. The director, playing the father would then ask him in a gentle voice, "What do you want from me?" The protagonist would respond by saying what it was that he wanted and the father figure would comply in the way requested by the protagonist. The idea was that the client would then have different feelings about the past incidents and be healed.

I had some training from the Philadelphia Psychodrama Institute in the late '80s and early '90s. I saw a man build a wall that represented barriers to achieving his goals while a classmate stood on the other side of the wall. The classmate symbolically represented success. The man built the wall with chairs, an end table, and a trash can. He kicked the props away and walked to success and shook her hand. The next time I encountered him, he shared that he was feeling much more confident about his chances for success.

Another time I got to play a young lady's abusive father. I sat and, as instructed, I gave her my most sarcastic laugh while pointing at her. She and a classmate grabbed me by each arm and angrily shoved me out of the door. A few minutes later, she called me back in and yelled at me. After she yelled at me, she altered my role by telling me what to say as if I had been a good father. I then played the good father. Later she reported that, although nothing changed in her relationship with her father, at least she no longer felt the anger and hostility towards him.

Based on these experiences, I have created an exercise which helps people resolve issues from their past memories by acting out a psychodrama in their head. Get ready to doctor the pain from past memories.

Exercise 3C—Doctoring the Pain from a Past Memory

You will need to find a room where you can be undisturbed for a half hour or more. Get your pen and journal, or your Word document.

1. Think of a memory that you have good and bad feelings about. Try to pick one that you did not use in the previous exercises.

2. Write the memory down with the same detail as you wrote in the other exercises, including sights, sounds, scents, feelings, and tastes. Refer to Exercise 1A for tips on recalling the details.

3. Write the beliefs you derived from the memory. Include the good beliefs and the negative beliefs.

4. Ask yourself, what about my memory would I like to be different? This could include how someone treated you, or what you could have done differently to handle the situation.

5. Close your eyes and relax each part of your body, beginning with your feet, then your legs, hips, stomach, torso, arms, hands, neck, face, and scalp. Breathe deeply.

6. Replay the memory that you wrote down in Step 1. Play it at your own pace the first time.

7. Now replay it at a fast pace.

8. Replay it a third time, but this time, replay it as if what you described in Step 4 actually occurred. For example, if you are working with a memory in which someone called you a nasty name, and you obviously would have preferred for them to say something nice to you, replay the event but change it such that the person actually said something nice to you.

9. Now imagine standing face to face with the person or persons who did something that you did not like.

10. First, imagine thanking them, but sarcastically. For example, thank a boss who fired you by saying thank you just like you would thank a police officer for giving you a ticket. Imagine their jaw dropping.

11. Then thank them for the experience and learning you derived from the memory. You can be sarcastic with this too. Imagine saying something to them like, "I learned from you that bigheaded people are not always right." Imagine them being the angry one now while you remain perfectly calm. Finally, thank them by being sincere about what you learned from the experience.

Since you have completed the exercises in this chapter, you now have some tools to help you change the way you feel about mixed and unhappy memories. You can try this on any memory that you often think about or any memory that bothers you.

As a Licensed Counselor who has helped hundreds of people change their beliefs about their memories, I can say that if a memory keeps coming to mind and you relive the upset, it means that you have not learned the lessons that it can teach. Besides, it takes effort to keep suppressing a memory, but when you no longer feel the emotional charge, the memory is less likely to keep surfacing.

Memories that you repeatedly think about are the ones that are the most important to resolve. Your mind is constantly trying to solve problems, and it will naturally remind you of problems that need to be resolved. There was an old expression that was popular a hundred years ago, **"The idle brain is the devil's playground."** When you are not controlling your thoughts, the thoughts that come will likely be about problems that are unresolved.

If memories of problems are the most important memories to resolve, which memories are the ones that shaped you the most and can teach you why you developed the way you did? In Chapter 4, you are going to explore which memories are important to you.

CHAPTER 4

What Negative Memories Or Issue Would You Like to Resolve?

Pitter patter goes the rain outside beating against our roof. The trees are sighing and rustling the few brown and yellow leaves that are still attached as the wind gets stronger.

In the living room, our new television is giving us a great example of the brilliant definition it is capable of displaying as we watch huge ocean waves smash fencing and quickly erode dunes in nearby Ventnor and Ocean City, New Jersey. The news broadcasters are standing right by the raging waves and telling us to go far away from where they are, and that there are no bridges available for any travelers to get out of the barrier islands.

What warriors those broadcasters are. What are their mothers, spouses, and children thinking as they watch them announce Super Storm Sandy's plans to smash into the Jersey shore tonight right where they are standing? The lights flicker in the house and my wife and mother-in-law gasp and comment that this might be it for our electricity.

Today and the next few days are going to easily gain a permanent stronghold in the memories of all people living on the east coast of the country. Not to mention the kids in the area who may have to forgo Halloween.

In my years of counseling, I have observed that people can be exposed to the same stimuli and have different reactions. Many people are terrified in a hurricane, blizzard, earthquake, or other natural disaster. They think that anyone who is not terrified either needs a sobriety test or they just don't know what is going on.

However, some people like adventure and are excited by the unknown and unusual. In a hurricane, they enjoy prepping their house with sandbags, filling the tub with water in case the toilet stops working, and making sure their flashlights have good batteries. Others enjoy going out and pushing cars to safety. Then there are those laid back people who will cheer that they don't have to go to work or to school and instead get out the remote control and the Xbox for a day or two of total relaxation.

You are the only person who has experienced your life in the way you have experienced it, and only you can know what issues and memories you need to resolve. Do not judge yourself as you heal your memories. If you have a particular memory or memories that need healing, accept that it is an issue for you. **My memories and issues are my own and I can recall them and heal them** is a useful belief to adopt.

Many of you already know what you want to work on and why you are reading this book. Others might know that they have memories that need healing but don't know how to begin. The next example will give you some ideas of memories or issues that you might knowingly or unknowingly have that you could resolve in order to be happier and more successful.

Example 5—Memories and Issues to Resolve

Is there something or someone that you are always complaining about? Is there a person such as a family member or a friend who you just can't get along with? Maybe your job drives you crazy and you can't seem to find anything good to say about it? Suppose you read this and thought, What will I pick? There are many things that I could complain about. Just pick one for the next exercise, and if it helps, go for the gold with all your complaints.

Is there any stress in your life that you feel you are not handling well? It could be that you have too much on your plate with work, school, and childrearing. Maybe your stomach tightens or your knee jerks when you hear or think of an additional task you have to do. Do you have memories of handling stress poorly?

Do you have trouble sticking to an exercise program? "Happy New Year everybody! My resolution is that I will lose fifty pounds this year, flatten my stomach, and be able to run a marathon." The memories of this year, last year, and the past ten years are as follows.

January—You started going to the gym. It was a long wait for each machine as many people seem to share your resolution.

February—Boy it's been a long winter. You need comfort food, even though you just finished your Valentine's Day candy. Your calendar says it's the 15th. That's right, it only took you a day to eat all of your Valentine's Day candy.

March—Well, you managed to hit the gym twice this month. It will be easier once winter is over.

April—It seems like an April fool's joke that you had that New Year's resolution. Then May starts the picnic and barbecue season with lots of outdoor parties all summer.

October—You are glad that you bought that leaf blower so it won't be such hard work raking the leaves.

December—You long ago gave up on the gym membership and purchased exercise equipment for your home. The treadmill however has Christmas balls and lights on it.

Surprise! It's January 1st, and time for you to repeat the cycle.

You may have some bad memories associated with physical fitness. Were you the last one picked for teams in gym class? Did your parents consider exercise much less important than school work? Is your family overweight?

Do you have unhealthy eating habits? Some of the same memories and attitudes towards exercise might be applied to this issue. Was food used for a reward when you were growing up? Did your mother put you on a diet and promise to reward you with a big chocolate cake when you lost ten pounds? Was food always a big part of every social event in which you were involved? Do you use comfort foods to make yourself feel better?

Do you have time management issues? Do you have memories of being late for everything? Have you ever joked that you would be late for your own funeral? Did you register for a time management seminar but then you were late for it? Do you frequently get frustrated that you did not get nearly as much accomplished in a day as you had hoped?

If you use poor time management as an issue for this exercise and you discover memories of having trouble concentrating in school, or asking people to repeat things that they just said, you may have Attention Deficit Disorder. There are medications, supplements, and coping techniques that can help you.

Are you stuck in a bad relationship? If you want a relationship or are unhappy with the one you are in, this is definitely an issue for you to explore. You may have already used a bad experience of this type with one of the previous exercises.

Do you disagree with your spouse or partner about how to parent your children? If you are raising children and you and your partner seem to disagree on disciplining them, where to send them to school, or what activities they should do, it might be helpful for you and your partner to recall memories of your own childhoods and how you were raised. When you both uncover your beliefs about childrearing, you can then reach compromises.

Are you a procrastinator? This issue is similar to the time management issue. If you habitually procrastinate it would be helpful to review occasions in which you have procrastinated in the past. How did you feel about completing the task at hand? Do you like to get started on things and get excited but then find them to be too much work? Are you afraid of completing things because then you will be judged as to whether or not you did a good job?

I have found that when I am working on a project, such as writing a book or developing a new therapy program for my clients, as weird as it sounds, that project can start to feel like a friend (the ceiling fan was an exception). This is because while I am working on a project, there is a voice in my head that is saying, "Okay, time to sit down and write," or, "Time for the meeting about the Anxiety Group."

When the project is complete, the voice is no longer there. Now I do not mean actually hearing a voice when no one is there. It is a thought that guides the work on the project and when the project is complete the voice is no longer there as a friend and guide.

This is why many middle aged people have trouble with what is known as Empty Nest Syndrome. For twenty or more years, they had the voice saying, "Time to make dinner," "Time to make lunches for tomorrow," "Time to do the evening bath routine." When the last child is out of the house, they not only miss their children but they miss the friendly voice telling them what to do. When I get a new empty nester in therapy, I always try to encourage them to volunteer their time somewhere, to start working, or to do something so they will have a goal to strive towards.

So what does this have to do with procrastination? When you procrastinate, the voice has to keep talking. Ironically, you might feel lonely when you finish your project because the voice will no longer be there.

I have observed among my clients and people I know personally that single people who live alone are often big procrastinators, particularly about cleaning their homes or apartments. Besides the obvious excuse that no one is there to nag them to clean up, I think they appreciate the company of that voice telling them to clean.

Do you avoid things out of fear? Is there anything that scares you? Maybe heights scare you, or ferrets, iPods, spiders with furry legs, confrontational people, hidden cameras, Jerusalem Artichokes, crowds, doing something klutzy in front of others? Whatever the fear may be, you have a memory or memories that created that fear. If you find the memory and then uncover subsequent memories of avoiding your fear, then it is no wonder you are still afraid. Avoiding a feared situation makes the fear stronger. Conversely, facing your fear helps to eliminate it.

There is a psychological technique used to combat fear called flooding. The therapist takes the client closer to the feared object and then floods the client with the stimulus (feared thing) until they are no longer afraid. Suppose the client is afraid of elevators. The therapist would bring the client to an elevator and ride with them. The client might be shaking and screaming at first, but they just keep riding the elevator until they are no longer afraid. Special precautions are taken so the client will not run out of the elevator when it stops at a floor. Emergency medical precautions are also taken as some people's fears can be quite intense and in some cases induce heart attacks or other serious medical conditions.

Do you often find yourself spending money to make yourself feel better? Have you ever bought something that afterwards you wished you could take back? Do you have memories that show a pattern of impulse buying? It would behoove you to think of your past purchases, what was happening to you, and how you were feeling immediately before you made the purchases.

Do you find yourself struggling with depression at certain times of the year? Do you have memories of being depressed at certain times of the year? Many people have a condition called Seasonal Affective Disorder or SAD. Typically, they become sad during the darker and colder times of the year from mid-November through February.

SAD has been attributed to the shorter days of the year when there is a lack of stimulation of the pineal gland.

This is the gland that helps the eyes perceive light. Doctors have prescribed special lamps that produce a certain wavelength of light which stimulates the pineal gland. The patient is advised to sit under the lamp for two or three hours a day during the dark hours of November through February.

I have seen clients and I have known people who were depressed at other times of the year, too, not just the dark days. The depression was due to losses, usually the death of a loved one, that occurred during that time of the year and then was later associated with that time of the year.

My grandmother used to feel good during autumn but would struggle with depression during the spring months. She had memories of gardening with her father in the spring and the spring depressions began after he died. Another woman I knew who was part of my circle of friends would disappear from the social scene every August. At first, we thought she was on vacation every year at that time, but eventually she explained that several of her family members had passed away during the month of August and she struggled with depression as she recalled those losses every August since. Recovering from a seasonal depression can involve finding positive beliefs about the time of year that brings the sadness. Recovering can also involve being grateful for the time that once was rather than being sad that it is over.

Do you struggle with anger? If you think about it, you will realize that there are two types of anger issues. Usually we think of anger as an inability to control one's temper. That is the first type of anger issue. If you don't have a problem with managing your anger, you might have in the past, or you might have memories of a significant person in your life that did have an issue. Maybe it was a parent, your romantic partner, or your boss.

The second type of anger issue is a fear of anger. Is there anyone who you behave very well around but you are not particularly comfortable being in their presence because they are usually an angry person? Are you one of those people who crosses every "t" in your job because you are deathly afraid of criticism and your boss becoming angry with you, so you try to be perfect? Maybe if you had a parent who yelled a lot and now your boss has a short fuse, you might be cautious and scared around him or her.

Feeling and expressing anger always comes from a specific way of thinking and perceiving things. My freshman philosophy teacher nailed it on Tuesday, October 31, 1978 when he said, "Anger comes when you think that someone is ripping you off." I thought about it and decided he was right.

As a freshman psychology student, I was curious about what thoughts and perceptions cause other feelings. I concluded that depression always comes from thoughts that life is no good. This can include thoughts that you won't get what you want, you don't have what you used to have, or that your present circumstances are not enjoyable or satisfying.

Anxiety comes from thoughts that something overwhelming is going to happen and you are not going to be able to handle it. Perhaps the fear of anger is also an anxiety issue. You feel anxious that your boss might yell at you. Consequently, when you hold the anxiety in long enough, you will sense that it is unfair for you to have to hold on to the anxiety, then you express anger instead.

Do you struggle to trust others? You will know if you have trust issues if you have a hard time making friends, if you get scared when you are getting close to someone, or if you push people away by obnoxious behavior.

Memories that can result in trust issues include being deserted by an adult you were close to when you were a child, a painful breakup, abuse from adults as a child, having been bullied in school, or any occurrence where you were disappointed.

Hurt feelings are close cousins to mistrust. Just as anger, anxiety, and depression have their origins in specific thoughts and perceptions, hurt stems from thoughts and expectations that someone would treat you in a loving way and they violated the unspoken or spoken agreement. Small hurts of this kind are typical in marriages. For example, a woman might verbalize to her husband that she doesn't want any gifts for her fortieth birthday. In her heart though, she may be beaming with excitement that he is going to get her a gift anyway because he cares about her and wouldn't want her to be gift-less on her birthday. He however, is a simple man, and took what she said at face value. Her birthday comes and he has no gift to give her. Her heart sinks as she starts to think that he doesn't care about her.

A small hurt could also take the form of a changed relationship. A young boy for example could grow up trusting his father and being close to him. As he gets older though, maybe his father becomes an alcoholic, and by the time the boy is thirteen years old, all those camping trips and nights out turn into occasions for physical and verbal abuse. He now may not trust people who treat him well and believe he is not worth anyone's time.

Example 5 listed common issues that perhaps are holding you back from success and happiness. We will now do an exercise which will define what is getting in the way of your success and happiness.

Exercise 4—This Is a Memory I Am Going to Heal

You will need a pen and your journal, or your Word document.

1. **Write in your journal any of the questions or examples from Example 5 that you became emotional about.**
2. **Write any thoughts that you had when you started reading this book that invoked strong emotion.**
3. **Answer the following questions:**

   • **When did I become anxious?**
   • **When did I become afraid?**

- When did I become sad?
- When did I become depressed?
- When did I become angry?

4. List the five best memories you have. You could probably refer to previous exercises to find them.
5. List the five worst memories you have.
6. Repeat Exercise 3B with the five worst.
7. If you get emotional about a past memory, do the relaxations from Exercise 3C.
8. If you still experience negative emotions from any memories identified within this exercise even though you've gone through the steps in Exercises 3B and 3C, write them down as a new list and title the new list, My Healing List.

You have now completed Exercise 4 and it's likely that you have a long list of issues you want to resolve. If you have a very long list, you may want to select no more than five memories to work on while you are going through the chapters of this book. Realize that you can continue to work on the exercises after you have completed reading the whole book. *Heal Your Memories, Change Your Life* is an excellent reference for you to use and return to throughout your life.

If you only had one or two issues, or you are still not sure what you want to work on, that could be good, too. It could mean that you are happy and well-adjusted and you can use these lessons to enrich your life. Most of the future chapters are designed to help you retrieve and heal memories from specific areas of your life. You may discover some memories and things that you had buried. A useful belief to adopt is that **anything you are able to learn can only help you.**

People differ not only in what memories and beliefs they have, but they differ in learning styles. The next chapter is a voyage to discover what your learning style is.

CHAPTER 5

Which Senses Do I Use the Most?

Do you *see* what I mean? I *hear* you. This just doesn't *feel* right. We all have individual ways of expressing ourselves. **People who say things such as, "Get the picture?" or, "I don't see the difference," are primarily visual people**. They see the world through pictures. These people often talk fast because they are trying to describe everything that they are seeing in their minds or in the world around them. Artists, photographers, and interior designers are primarily visual people.

Then there are people who are primarily auditory. They think and interpret the world through sounds. I hear you. This isn't clicking with me. That sounds good. These are common ways auditory learners express themselves. Musicians, singers, and actors and actresses are auditory people. If you have ever listened to a great speech where the orator had a great speaking voice, he or she was probably an auditory learner.

I feel like this is right. This isn't sitting right with me. These are the battle cries of the kinesthetic learners. These people are more attuned to their bodies. Athletes, and massage practitioners, and highly emotional people are kinesthetic learners. It is no accident that the word "feel" applies to bodily sensations and emotions. Some old expressions related to temperature such as, **"You are going to be in hot water," and, "I get a cold feeling around him," were likely coined by kinesthetic people**. Since athletes are kinesthetic, the term "warm up" is used before a game. Warm up can also be used in an emotional sense to mean that you are getting comfortable around someone with whom you had an emotionally uncomfortable experience.

Although everyone has a sense they use more than others, most people have a secondary sense that they use almost as much. I know a man who has a construction business (a kinesthetic job) but is also a talented artist. His house has pictures and murals on the walls of God and Jesus. He has some abstract art which includes a picture of my wife's hand with parts of other objects. In Exercise 5, you will determine what your main and secondary senses are and how you can apply this to accessing memories and to change your life.

The other two senses are olfactory and gustatory. Olfactory is your sense of smell, and gustatory is your sense of taste. There are some people who have highly developed olfactory or gustatory senses.

People who create and manufacture perfumes have a strong olfactory sense. Cooks and chefs have a strong gustatory sense and are able to distinguish subtle differences in spices and additives for foods. If you enjoy watching Chopped, you might be someone with a strong gustatory sense.

If you are always telling yourself that you eat too much and need to diet, should you forget about dieting and use the excuse that you have a strong gustatory sense? No, food actually tastes better when you eat it in moderation.

In Chapter 1, there was mention of comfort foods, which are foods that soothe the nerves. If you are eating excessive amounts of pizza and chocolate, you may be looking more to calm your nerves than to satisfy your gustatory sense. You will fare better doing the exercises in this book.

Although olfactory is not known to be one of the main senses people have, I will informally conclude that smells and scents bring back memories and feelings more effectively than pictures and songs.

Have you ever revisited a place that you frequented in your past and memories came flooding back when you inhaled a unique scent from that place? Maybe you go to an old hotel that you vacationed in as a child and the scent of a flower they use in the lobby or the cleaning agent they use in the rooms brings back a flood of memories. Aromas have been used to help people with Alzheimer's recall memories.

Understanding your learning style can be very useful in your relationships. I have used this next exercise frequently in my work with couples who are having problems communicating. Often people who have different primary senses have trouble communicating because it is as if they do not speak each other's language.

If the wife is saying, "I see you are not listening again," and the husband responds with, "I feel that is unfair," they are not going to understand each other. If they aren't going to understand each other, then they will not meet each other's wants and needs. Can you see (or hear, or feel) from this example that she is visual and auditory and he is kinesthetic?

I have seen couples improve their communication and their marital satisfaction by tuning into each other's styles. When I give them the exercise you are about to complete, it helps them understand each other better.

There are standardized tests that have proven to help people determine their dominant learning style. However, I prefer to use the exercise that I have used to help my clients because, as I mentioned in the introduction, I want to make this experience as personal as possible for you. Let's get started!

Exercise 5—What Is My Learning Style?

You will need a pen and your journal, or your Word document. Hopefully you will be able to set aside an hour of your time for this.

1. **Pick a memory that is vivid for you, preferably a significant event that you remember a lot about, most people choose a graduation, their wedding day, the birth of a child, or a memorable vacation. This is the only exercise where you will be asked to pick a memory that you do not want or need to improve your recall as done in previous exercises. You should remember this memory naturally.**

2. **Write as many details as you can recall. Take your time with this and just write until you have nothing more to write. Since you are becoming a seasoned**

expert at recalling memories, you may start writing and be flooded with a lot details about the event. This is good because the idea here is to get as many details as possible.

3. Start a new page and make three columns. In column one, at the left of the page, write Visual at the top. In the middle column, write Auditory, and in the right column, write Kinesthetic.

4. Review your description of the event. Write any words that describe visual cues in the left column. This includes anything you saw, descriptions of scenery, how people were dressed and what you wore, anything that met your eyes.

5. Review your description again. Look for any descriptions of things you heard. It could be music, a conversation, the sigh of traffic, anything that you remember hearing. Count each thing you heard as one entry.

6. Review your description a third time. This time, note anything you felt physically or emotionally. Maybe it was a day at the beach and you remember feeling the sand on your feet. You might remember getting angry at someone or feeling love for someone.

7. Now add your totals for each column. If you scored highest in the Auditory column, then it is likely that you are an auditory learner. You are attuned to sound. You probably like music and the sounds of nature, and you are more than likely a good listener.

If you scored highest on Kinesthetic in the third column, then you are probably attuned to your body and can get emotional over things. This is okay. It will guide you in your future life decisions. If you scored highest on visual, you need to do some basic math before being able to say for sure that you are a visual learner. Your Visual score in column one needs to be at least twice as high as your second highest score in either of the other two columns. For example, if you had twenty visual cues and thirteen auditory cues, then you are probably auditory as thirteen plus thirteen equals twenty-six which is more than twenty. However, if you had thirty visual cues and only thirteen auditory cues, then you are probably visual as thirty is more than twice as high as thirteen. There are many more visual cues in the world so there is more to perceive.

Since you have now completed Exercise 5, you have a good idea of which sense is your strongest. Naturally, the sense that you scored second highest on is your second best. In Chapter 6, we will look at some of your earliest memories which we will use later to help identify more about who you are.

When you combine learning style with personality type, and any other information that you can learn about yourself, that information can be a compass for decisions you make in your future. These decisions can lead to choosing the right career, the right life partner, and making right decisions in your life because you will have all the facts! The next couple of chapters will help to uncover memories and beliefs that make you who you are today.

CHAPTER 6

What Are Your Earliest Memories?

"Okay Child Psychology class, today we are going to look back in time, back to your earliest memory. In our last class, I asked you to think about what your earliest memory is. If you didn't know, you were allowed to ask your parents to give you some ideas." **I then explain to them the theory of infantile amnesia. It's the idea that no one can remember anything before age three because the brain is not sufficiently developed.**

This class activity was an experiment of sorts. After explaining the theory, I went around the room and asked half of the students what their earliest memory was, and how old they were when it happened. I rarely got an answer below age three. Then I would explain that I remember singing the song "Moon River" with my mother. She confirmed that I was a year and a half when I sang that song with her. I also remember Christmas morning when I was two, sitting up in my crib while my parents demonstrated how to play with my toys before they took me out of my crib so I could play with them myself.

When I was finished sharing these memories with the class, I went around the rest of the room to ask the remainder of the students what their earliest memory was and how old they were when it happened. Interestingly, after I shared my earliest memories that contradicted the theory of infantile amnesia, there were more students who answered that their earliest memory occurred while they were between two and three years old.

Although there were differences in the professed ages of the students in the first and second half of the activity, the quality of the memories remained the same. Every memory was an event that would be considered by most people to be out of the ordinary.

Example 6—First Memories

- **I remember my dad taking me in his truck to deliver bread one time.**
- **I remember being at the community pool and falling on the concrete around the pool.**
- **I remember being taken on a plane.**
- **I remember going to visit my grandparents.**
- **I remember having sand thrown in my face.**

What would you say are the common denominators of these memories? They are events that do not happen every day, and they are emotionally charged. We tend to remember events that have high emotional charge

because our brain tells us they are important. Note that the intensity of the emotion was quite high in these experiences regardless of whether the experience was happy or unhappy.

The boy who was taken with his dad on his dad's bread route was provided with good father and son bonding time and this attention made the boy feel special. The fall that the other boy experienced on the concrete at the pool made a normally fun experience painful. At a young age, a plane ride is a unique experience and could be thrilling or scary. A young girl who had sand thrown in her face probably is not a beach lover now unless she was able to heal that painful experience.

The students' perception of the age of their earliest memory was influenced by me sharing my own memories. They may have wanted to believe that they remembered more or maybe they wanted to impress the teacher. It is conceivable that the recall of the details of the memories was not one hundred percent accurate, but they remembered the incident because it was significant and novel to them.

Some psychologists believe that a person's earliest memories are the most influential and shape their personality and tendencies more than later childhood, adolescent, and adult memories. It is possible that this is correct. However, I do not subscribe to the idea that permanent damage is done by any early childhood memory. It will be useful and it is possible to learn how to change any beliefs from early childhood memories even if those beliefs were formed at an early age. If you have any longstanding beliefs that are not helping you, changing them can be powerful and freeing.

You are becoming an old pro at healing your memories. In Chapter 2, you learned how to identify the beliefs you have formed based on your past memories. In Chapter 4, you defined what issues you want to work on, and in Chapter 5, you identified your learning style. Now it's time to put your skills to work and further your learning.

In Exercise 6A, you are going to dissect your earliest memories to identify how your early childhood experiences are affecting you now. Example 7 will give you an idea of how the next exercise will work.

Example 7—The Patterns of Your Early Memories

Suppose that your earliest memory was having surgery when you were three years old. You remember your parents bringing you to the hospital, and your mother holding your hand as the doctor sedated you. Shortly after waking up, you remember having your favorite food followed by some ice cream. You also remember your parents and grandparents at your bedside the whole time.

You also might remember the time when you were five years old and you couldn't catch your breath and were gasping for air. Your father did not want to wait for the paramedic so he took you to the hospital in the car. You remember speeding down the road and other cars honking their horns at your dad for disobeying the rules of the road as he runs through three red lights. When you arrived at the hospital, he stood by your bed the entire time.

Then at six, you fell and broke your ankle playing in your first Pee Wee Soccer game. You were disappointed that you couldn't play soccer anymore, but the injury was worth the attention you got from your parents as they waited on you hand and foot. You also thoroughly enjoyed all the kids at school gawking at your injury and lining up to autograph your cast.

What about memories of times that you were not sick or injured? Sure, you have some, but you seem to more easily recall times when you received preferential treatment and everyone's undivided attention because you were sick or injured. Is this why at age twenty-three, you always want to go to the hospital for even the smallest cut on your finger?

There is a theme running through the events in Example 7—being given excessive and preferential attention when sick or injured. This theme may have led to a belief that when you are sick or injured, you receive excessive love and attention. Here are some other examples showing how themes through childhood might form beliefs.

- **A child whose parents always praised them whether it was for their first step, toilet training, or strapping** themselves into their own car seat might now believe that achievement leads to love and recognition.

- A child who was always bullied in grade school now might have low self esteem and believe that they aren't worth anything to anyone.
- A child who always got upset when they saw pictures of poor and starving people on television, and would always cry when someone else cries might now believe that people need their help.

Sometimes, people will subconsciously start acting in a way opposite of how they were taught as a means of protesting against their experiences, such as explained in the next set of examples.

- A child who received so much attention from adults that they felt like they never had a minute to themselves might now prefer to be alone or prefer to be with animals instead of people. They may beleive that they are an introvert and that other people are annoying.
- A child who was raised in an authoritarian, military family might now believe that they are happier doing nothing than working hard.
- A child who was raised in a permissive environment where there was no discipline might believe that there are no rules in life.

Now that you have seen how themes lead to beliefs in Example 7, let's do an exercise to find your earliest memory and identify any beliefs formed from themes in your childhood.

Exercise 6A—What Is Your Earliest Memory?

You will need your pen and journal, or your Word document.

1. **What is your earliest memory? Use the same techniques you used in Exercise 1. You may start recalling more details than you thought you could. However, noticing a lot of detail at a young age is difficult so there may not be a lot of detail for you to recall.**

2. **Note if any similar memory came to mind as you pondered the first memory. Write what you remember about that similar memory. Continue this as more memories surface.**

3. **Look at your list of early memories. Is there a pattern to the memories you had and the way you behaved?**

4. **Repeat Exercise 6A with the list of memories you found. You do not need to go through each one, especially if they were similar.**

5. **List any beliefs you may have formed based on your list of memories. Include beliefs about yourself, other people, and the world.**

Now that you have completed this exercise, you know what beliefs you have formed in early childhood. Beliefs that are acquired when you are that young are often deeply ingrained. Now we are going to take this a step further. Let's see how your present tendencies may be traced back to that early conditioning.

Example 8—Behaviors and Tendencies Based on the Past

We are going to take the previous examples of events and see examples of behaviors that could develop from them.

1. **Believing that you receive more preferential treatment when you are sick rather than healthy could lead to a condition known as hypochondria. This is when someone is obsessed with illness or injury and always thinks that something is wrong with them. A hypochondriac may want to be taken to the hospital for any minor injury, such as a small cut.**

2. **The person who was bullied in school and now believes that they aren't worth anything might always take the blame for things at work or at home even when it isn't their fault. Alternatively, some people who are bullied become bullies themselves.**

3. The person who got upset when they saw pictures of starving children and believes that the world needs their help might grow up to work for Save the Children, or they might join the Peace Corps.

4. The person who received relentless attention as a child and now believes himself or herself to be an introvert could grow up to become a quiet loner who likes dogs better than people.

5. The person who grew up in the authoritarian, military style family and now believes they are happier when they aren't working hard might grow up to be a free spirit who floats from job to job to jail to job to youth hostel to spouse to divorce.

6. The person who grew up with permissive parents and now believes that there are no rules might grow up to become an alcoholic or a drug addict.

Exercise 6B—What Tendencies Do You Have?

You will again need a pen and your journal. For this exercise, if you have been using a Word document, get some drawing paper and crayons or markers. Since this is about childhood memories, let's have some fun!

1. Look over your answers to Exercise 6A. Pay special attention to your answers in Steps 3, 4, and 5 of Exercise 6A.

2. Now think of any tendencies you have towards extreme behavior. Do you prefer to be alone? Do you like to go out? Are you active or are you easygoing?

3. Imagine that you are a small child riding a train that has three station stops. The first station is Memory Lane Station, the second station is Belief Ville, and the third station is Personality Point. Draw a train and some tracks. (I did this myself and my drawing skills are stick-man level. Don't be discouraged if your drawing skills are less than that of an artist. Give it a try anyway!) Draw three boxes along the tracks to represent the stations and name them with the aforementioned headings. In Memory Lane Station, list the memory or memories you used for exercise 6A. If you found common elements of multiple memories, list the elements. In Belief Ville, list the beliefs that you identified in Exercise 6A, Step 5. In the third station, Personality Point, list things about yourself. You can start with the traits you listed in Step 2. If you feel really creative today, you can list more then what you identified in Step 2.

Since you have now completed Exercise 6B, you have a pictorial representation of yourself and the tendencies you developed in childhood, plus you got in touch with your inner child! Keep that information as we move to the next chapter.

CHAPTER 7

Memories from School-What Did You Excel In?

It was a hot sunny day in the middle of the hottest summer of my life up to that point—Wednesday, July 27, 1988. I was helping my parents move into a new house. Survival strategies were in order. My game plan for avoiding the chaos was to be on the road as often as possible hauling everything I could fit in the cab of my red midsized Ford Ranger Pickup from the old house to the new house.

By three in the afternoon, I felt that I needed a break. I was alone in the new house after unloading the latest cargo of belongings. Included was a milk crate filled with old report cards. I saw one of mine from sixth grade which contained a comment. "Frank puts good ideas into carelessly prepared reports. He is smart and creative but disorganized." The report card was dated Friday, April 7, 1972.

Now, sixteen years later, I had just completed my first year of graduate school. I recalled on Monday, April 25, I received a term paper back with two grades on it:

"Content A, Format C." I chuckled inwardly that I really hadn't changed much in sixteen years.

Other school memories began flooding into my brain. In first grade, I remembered my music teacher saying that I was the best music student in his class. I don't know what happened between that time and the later story I shared where I had to face the band director in high school.

In second grade, the gym teacher told my parents that I did great back flips. It appears that my minimal athletic talent consisted of back flips, volleyball, and catching baseballs when they were hit right into my glove. Typically in gym class, I was one of the bargaining chips that others used for getting a good athlete. "You can have this one if you take Healy." "No, don't give the ball to Healy, he never scores."

In third grade, I found a car ad in a magazine that had three men and one woman who looked like they were up to no good. The photo inspired me to write a short story about gangsters. My teacher was so impressed that she called my mother in for a conference and told her to continue encouraging my creativity.

In fifth grade, I was chosen to be the announcer for an end of the year event called Color Day. Color Day was a fancy name for Field Day. They must have figured that they would use my talent for speaking instead of risking my athleticism. Despite an alleged talent for speaking, during the same year I was sent weekly to see the speech therapist in the school, go figure!

On Tuesday, May 30, 1972, my sixth grade teacher asked me what source I used to plagiarize a poem about nouns, verbs, and pronouns. I insisted (which was true) that I made it up as part of the assignment she had given us. "Well anyone who can write this must have poetry buzzing around their brain and everywhere else. Please read it to the class." I proudly read the poem to the class and received genuine applause.

Seventh grade was more difficult. One day, the kids decided that because of my handwriting, I was going to be a doctor. They told my English teacher about my handwriting, Mrs. Deardorf, who once said, "I would hate to have him. He would probably wrap my appendix in a gym sock." However, by the end of that year, Mrs. Deardorf had taught me the value of hard work and I became a good student with marginal organizational skills.

Eighth grade was pure scholarship. I remember my Social Studies teacher picked on everyone. However, I liked him because he picked on me about being smart. Other students cut his classes because he was giving them a hard time.

By the end of high school, I believed that I was smart, creative, caring, and compassionate. I retained the beliefs from grade school that I was not athletic. Socially I was always quiet. Any friends that I had were kids who reached out to me. I believed that I was meant to be a quiet person. Although I believed this, I did not like it. Throughout my school years there were kids who I would have liked to know but I was too shy to reach out to them.

As many people are especially shy when they meet a member of the opposite sex that they like, I could barely talk to girls. In college, I decided that I had had enough of this. I started talking to people I passed on the sidewalks, and I started going to parties. I changed my belief about being the quiet kid and decided I was an outgoing and friendly person and have been one all of my adult life.

Then it was time to graduate from college and face the world. In college, I enjoyed psychology, philosophy, and religion courses the most. Perhaps it was the discovery of abstract thinking that changed my academic interests from facts to theories. I also began putting more effort into fitness. On most days, I would take time to swim in the Olympic sized pool at La Salle University.

My first life lesson in the post college work world was that working with teenagers was not my forte. This was followed by several jobs working with developmentally disabled people. Although I connected well with them, I did not have a lot of patience with the slow pace or the silly salaries in that field.

Teaching seemed like a good gig in the late '80s, so I started the Elementary Education program at Temple University. At the start of the second year, I did fieldwork in a grade school near the campus. The teacher had me run a reading group in a third grade class of kids with learning difficulties. We were to learn the letter "G" and review words that began with it. I was on a roll. After about ten minutes, they all seemed to have mastered the letter "G" so I moved on to "H" and "I".

After the class regrouped, there was a short review session and they were sent to lunch. Filled with pride and excitement, I practically floated to the front of the room and beamed as I explained to the teacher that I had taught the kids three letters. My educational triumph, however, was short lived. The teacher explained that that group of students spends two weeks on each letter. I decided then that Elementary Education was too slow for me.

Eventually, I transferred to Chestnut Hill College and their graduate Counseling Psychology Program. I have been saving the world one patient at a time ever since.

Now it's your turn to write your life story. Don't worry about grammar, penmanship, or spelling. This exercise is for you to recount your school days, including college, graduate school, or trade school, and to make some discoveries about what you are good at and what you like doing.

Exercise 7—School Days

You will need a pen and your journal, or your Word document. It will be useful to find memorabilia from school, including old report cards, artwork, papers, trophies, school pictures. Go on your Facebook page and Classmates.com if you belong to either of those networking sites and look at old stories and pictures that your old schoolmates have posted.

1. **Organize your memorabilia by grade if that is feasible.**

2. **Write down everything that you can remember about elementary school, middle school, high school, and college. Have fun with this. It can be fun to recall your school days—the good as well as the bad.**

3. **You may find that after you complete your original writing, more memories will surface later in the day or over the next few days. There is no need to hurry to complete this exercise, you can always add to your story.**

4. **When you feel that you have enough information, make four lists. If you do this exercise on paper, you could tear a page out of your journal and divide it into four squares. If you are doing it electronically, you could do this exercise in Excel and divide a worksheet into four columns.**

5. **The four lists you make will be drawn from the autobiography you just wrote. The categories are Activities I Liked Doing, Activities I Was Good At Doing, Activities I Did Not Like Doing, and Activities I Was Not Good At Doing. Go through your life story and separate events into these categories.**

6. Go down each of the four lists and see if there is any change between your school days and now. For example, is there something you did not like doing in your school years but you like doing now? Is there something you are good at now that you were not good at then? Maybe you were never good in math but became interested when you got into the work world and started making money, now you are very good at managing money and consequently, good at math. Maybe you were good at sports but now, unfortunately due to illness or injury, you can't perform any strenuous physical activities. If that is the case, then this activity might help you rediscover what you can still do.

7. Review the information that you listed in all four columns. This should give you a strong idea of how you can live your life now. If you are thinking of making a career change, this could guide you in your choices. If you are someone who has a lot of free time, recalling these memories could give you an idea of how to spend your time.

8. If you recalled a traumatic memory from doing this exercise, follow the steps in Exercise 4 to heal yourself of negative emotions from the memory.

9. If you find that you do not have anything in the Activities I Liked Doing or Activities I Was Good At Doing columns, ask yourself the following questions.

- **Is there something you were good at doing, but maybe you didn't credit for doing it?**
- **Is there anything you used to do besides the things you didn't like or weren't good at doing?**
- **Are you discrediting what you were good at doing (thinking it does not matter)?**

If at any time you feel that you need professional help with the issues that surface while recalling any memories, you can consult my website: www.phenomenalmemory.com. It has articles and resources to further your learning.

Probably the worst memories that people recall from school are incidents of being bullied. Since the Columbine High School shooting in 1999, there has been much publicity about bullying. However, the efforts that have been made to prevent bullying have fallen short as it seems to be more prevalent in schools today than it ever was. In the next chapter, we will focus on overcoming the memories and the effects of bullying.

CHAPTER 8

Let's Put the Bullies in the Past

For six years, Kate's life was a living nightmare. This teen girl with a roundish face and long straight brown hair was tormented by kids in her middle school and high school who constantly called her **ugly and disgusting, and a host of other names which were far from flattering. It was an endless ordeal.**

In middle school, Kate would retaliate by calling the bullies names. However, such incidents would always end in a trip to the principal's office where the faculty of the school would not side with her, but instead would give her a lecture about how retaliation is never the answer. The other girls who made Kate's life a nightmare were never reprimanded. Finally, Kate decided to stop retaliating as it only seemed to make things worse for her. **Kate now felt that she had no protection as the faculty of the school never rescued her from her tormentors.**

High school brought more creative forms of bullying. Girls who were not her friends passed her notes that read, **"Kill yourself. No one wants you here anyway."** Girls who were allegedly her friends would walk away from the lunch table when the bullies approached, leaving her alone with her tormentors and her gloomy thoughts. **Kate often thought of suicide and would cry in her room after school, seeing no way out of her horrific life.**

The realization that her suicide would hurt her parents was the only factor that prevented her from killing herself. Perhaps surprisingly, Kate never told her parents what was going on at school. It was not that they would not have helped. They were supportive and always told her that she was a great person. But for some reason, Kate believed that she was supposed to be able to handle things herself, including the bullying. One night at dinner, she told her parents that she would like to be transferred to the local Catholic School. Her mother expressed confusion and asked Kate why she suddenly wanted to leave her friends. Kate dropped the matter not wanting to get into any detail of her situation and never brought it up again.

Many of you probably have memories of your parents complementing you when you were a teenager. If you had a history like Kate, your response probably fell along the range of rejecting the complements to questioning their intelligence and sanity. By the age of fourteen or fifteen, Kate had heard how ugly and disgusting she was so many times that she told her mother to stop telling her how great she was. Kate couldn't believe that the nice things her mother said were true given the horrible things she had been hearing from her schoolmates on a daily basis for years. **Most teenagers draw their beliefs from what their schoolmates tell them and do not place much credence in what their parents say. Consequently, Kate continued to believe that she was disgusting and ugly.**

Not only did the nasty remarks continue in high school, but some untrue rumors were also being spread about Kate. **Boys that Kate did not know were spreading lies that she had slept with them. There was even a rumor that she had slept with the English teacher, and the whole varsity football team.** How ironic, a girl who was so ugly and disgusting sure could get the men. It just did not make any sense. When she was not being accused of sleeping with boys and teachers, she was being beat up by other girls.

One would think that going home at the end of the school day would be a relief for Kate, but this wasn't the case. After school hours, there was cyber bullying. **Classmates would fabricate stories on fake MySpace pages and spread anonymous rumors. The rumors were similar to what was being spread at school about Kate sleeping with boys and teachers.**

Who were these kids who bullied Kate all through school? Were they the lady jocks? Were they the ones that dressed Goth? Were they the druggies? No, many of these kids were the good girls who dressed well, held offices in the school, and were the teacher's pets. **Consequently, in any dispute, the teachers would not side with Kate, just as the principal did not take her side in middle school.**

In the previous chapter, we discussed how your beliefs change as you go through grade school, middle school, and high school, and how your abilities change and develop in concert with those beliefs. Hopefully you were able to clear any negative and unrealistic beliefs that you previously had, and hopefully you are able to move on to a better life now. Despite believing that she was socially unappealing, Kate was able to retain the belief that she was smart. She managed to get good grades throughout school. She toyed with the idea of running for class offices but doubted that she would be elected and thought the visibility would cause her more problems.

Then it was time for college. Kate went to a college in a neighboring state which was a three hour drive from her home town. College seemed surreal to her at first. People were being nice to her and it took her time to accept it. She made friends easily, but she found it difficult to fully trust anyone. If anyone told her that a certain boy liked her, she wouldn't believe them as this had been done to her as a joke in middle school and she assumed it was the same thing.

As time went on, Kate changed her beliefs about herself and made some new life decisions based on her new self-image. **She decided that she was tired of feeling like an ugly, disgusting person when there was no evidence in her current environment to warrant it. She was also tired of feeling bad in general.**

Out of an act of will, she adopted the beliefs that she was beautiful and confident, deserving of happiness, and

intelligent. With these new beliefs, she made a decision to be who she was regardless of what anyone else thought of her. She ran for several offices and won, including President of her Junior Class and President of the National Honor Society Chapter in her school.

Kate is now a very happy, well-adjusted twenty something. She has an engaging manner, and new friends. She laughs easily and appreciates everything in her life. There is no evidence that she has been permanently traumatized by her past.

Besides changing her beliefs about herself, she forgave everyone. Motivated by the desire to live a happy and successful life, she decided it was not worth holding on to the past. She would say, "The bullies were people whose minds were not fully developed." Kate shared that when she encounters many of the former bullies in her home town, they are polite and say hi to her as if the past had never happened. **"It was just a dark time in my life,"** says Kate with conviction that that time is now over.

When Kate first gained notoriety as an anti-bullying activist, she received a plethora of letters from young adults who had been bullied in school. Ironically, she heard from a lady who had been a schoolmate of hers and who she thought was a popular kid. The schoolmate shared that she had been bullied too and had many other problems. You just never know!

Kate's story is inspirational. If all that it takes to recover from bullying memories is to change your beliefs about yourself and about the bullies, to decide that you want to be happy, to put the past behind you, and to forgive them, then let's get to it.

Exercise 8A—Put Bullying in the Past

You will need a pen and your journal, or your Word document. You will also need your pictures and memorabilia from Exercise 7.

1. **Look through your journal from previous exercises, particularly from the last chapter on school memories. Think of your interactions with your schoolmates. If you did not include those interactions, reading your journal and looking at pictures can trigger memories of interactions. Write some short narratives of interactions you had. You can include good as well as bad interactions.**

2. **List at least two positive, happy experiences you had in school. Even if you were someone who was a top student and had only two friends all through school, there had to have been some good experiences. They can include good times at recess, lunch, activities such as soccer or band, playing with friends on weekends, dates, bringing a friend on a family vacation, or any other happy time.**

3. **Repeat Steps 5 and 6 of Exercise 4. Relax and enjoy the memory.**

4. Now pick a not so pleasant memory. Some suggestions include being ridiculed in gym class if you were not good in sports, being ridiculed if you got an answer wrong in class, someone making a joke that someone else liked you when they really didn't like you, being called ugly, wimpy, or any other variation of the "too's" such as too tall or too short. It could be the unpleasant memory of a student grabbing your term paper and tearing it up (in the old days, there was no hard drive to save information), or the time you were in college being harassed by a fraternity or a sorority.

5. Think about what you thought of yourself when that memory happened. You may have adopted a belief that you are ugly, or that you bring disgrace to whatever organizations you belong to, or that you are not as good as other people.

6. Visualize the good memories again, the same as you did in Exercise 4. When you are feeling your best from visualizing the good memories, begin to then visualize the bad memory. Only spend a brief amount of time on the bad memory, less than thirty seconds, then pick a good memory and visualize it in more detail than you did the bad memory. When you are ready, open your eyes.

7. Notice how you feel about the bullying memory. It is probable that you do not feel as intense as you did

before. You can now look at the memory with more objectivity.

8.   Refer to your list of beliefs from Step 5. Ask yourself the following questions.

- Can I learn anything from this incident?
- Are any of these negative beliefs that I have still relevant?
- If they are not relevant, what can I now believe instead?

9.   Ask yourself if there is any life lesson you can learn from this memory.

If you had trouble with the last exercise, specifically with lowering the intensity of the emotion from the bullying memory, you may have not spent enough time imagining the good memory. The idea in the visualization was to feel good remembering the good episode, so that the good feeling will lower the intensity of the sad or angry feeling when you remember the bullying. However, if you became intensely angry, sad, or anxious when you remembered the bullying, it may be that you are good at focusing in the present moment.

If you get too upset over the memories, I would advise you to skip the visualizations about unhappy memories. Your recall of them is probably intense enough without visualizing. You can focus on the belief changing techniques instead.

Frequently in my counseling practice, I assign my patients to journal their thoughts when they are feeling angry, depressed, or anxious. They are advised to journal after the experience as they are often too upset to think clearly and write when they are having a panic attack, a crying spell, or an angry outburst.

Patients often report back to me at their next session that the journaling helped them feel less intense about the experience. This holds true whether they were writing about an experience they had that morning or something that happened twenty years ago. The act of writing out their thoughts and feelings gives them a sense of control, and makes them feel as though the thoughts and feelings are no longer in their heads but outside of themselves as they gaze down at the journal and observe what they have written.

Exercise 8B—Getting It out of Your System

You will need to sit in a quiet place where you will be undisturbed. Bring a pen and your journal, or your Word document.

1. **Think of a past memory of being bullied. If nothing comes to mind, look through your pictures and previous journal entries. If you honestly have no memories of being bullied, it is okay to skip this exercise.**

2. **Quickly begin writing about the experience. Just keep writing until you don't have anything else to say about it. Don't dwell too long as you may become overly emotional.**
3. **Pick a pleasant interaction that you had with someone recently. It could be with a friend, a coworker, or a family member. Relax and close your eyes. Imagine the experience similar to the way you visualized a good experience in Exercises 2A and 8A. Just let it come!**
4. **When you are ready, open your eyes. You should be feeling good now. Take as much time as you need to reorient yourself.**
5. **Look down at your journal again. Tell yourself that what you have written is not the current or the recent reality. It is no longer what you are experiencing but a distant memory. It is no longer who you are.**

After you have completed this exercise, you are probably feeling better. You may be feeling grateful for the experience you just visualized, and the bullying memory may even seem surreal. If you liked this exercise, you can use it for any previous memory that you would like to forget, or at least eliminate the feelings that you get when the memory surfaces.

After healing the emotions associated with any history you may have of being bullied, it may also be necessary for you to review the beliefs you have formed from incidents of bullying in order to revise those beliefs as Kate did when she was in college. In an earlier chapter, you learned that beliefs are conclusions you have drawn about life. They are based on your past experiences. However, you can change those beliefs with or without evidence. Example 9 should help you to get started.

Example 9—Useful Beliefs about Past Bullying

- **When I was younger, I was more vulnerable than I am now. Now I can be confident.**
- **I respect myself, so I will be respected.**
- **The people who bullied me had undeveloped minds.**
- **If it was more than seven years ago, they and I are not even in the same bodies.**
- **What the bullies did to me says everything about them and nothing about me.**
- **It didn't kill me, so I am stronger.**

The first belief, **when I was younger, I was more vulnerable,** shows you that now you are a different person in different surroundings. It is likely that you have more confidence as you have grown and have handled more situations and have developed more skills than you had before. However, you might not have acknowledged that you are now a different person if you have a tendency to not give yourself credit for your accomplishments. If you think hard enough, you can find many reasons why you and your life are different now than when you were bullied.

I respect myself, so I will be respected. In recent years the popularity of the Law of Attraction has caused people to believe that they create their reality from the inside. I do believe that the Law of Attraction is a law of nature. The field of psychology agrees that you will be treated according to the demeanor that you project. So if you treat yourself with respect, including acknowledging your good points, accepting yourself warts and all, and presenting yourself to the world with confidence which comes from the inside, you will get more respect than if you present yourself like a scared rabbit who expects to be bullied.

The people who bullied me had undeveloped minds. Studies have shown that the brain does not reach maturity until around age twenty, and even then, some parts are still not completely matured until the late twenties. Given this late development, children and teenagers often have limited capacity to understand what bullying does to others. Their self-esteem is undeveloped too and they try to boost it by devaluing and ridiculing others.

Science has now concluded that our bodies replace themselves every seven years. Naturally the air, food, and liquid inside of us are replaced more frequently. However, you can give yourself a good laugh by concluding that the body you have and the body that the bullies have now are not at all the same bodies as when the bullying occurred.

Now we go from biology to philosophy—imagine **that you see someone on the street or in a bar or a restaurant bullying another person**. Do you think less of the person who is being bullied or do you think less of the bully? I took a recent poll and between seventy and eighty percent of the people said they would think less of the bully. It is a useful belief that the bullies were just weak characters and that you are okay.

Finally, give yourself a pat on the back and take out that iPod or MP3 player loaded with Kelly Clarkson's "Stronger" set to repeat. You survived the bullying so now you are a stronger person.

Let's elaborate on the idea that the bullies were people with undeveloped minds and undeveloped character. **Given that you understand this aspect of biology, you can forgive them, and it will help you put the offenses behind you and forgive the people who hurt you. Forgiveness is often taught as a necessary action in order for you to be recognized as a nice person. However, forgiveness seems to be a mandate without a manual.** We are supposed to forgive, but we are not taught how. For this reason, I am going to discuss what forgiveness is and is not.

Example 10—Forgiveness

Forgiveness is not:

- **Deciding that what the person did to you was okay.**
- **Acknowledging that the offender is a great person.**
- **Inviting them over for dinner.**

- **Bragging about how great you are because you forgave.**
- **Expecting something back from them to compensate for the offense.**
- **Waiting until something happens in life so what happened does not matter.**

Forgiveness is:

- **Letting go of hurt and anger. You feel no more feelings about the offense.**
- **Letting go of blame, including blaming them for the way you turned out.**
- **Not expecting or wanting anything back from the person.**
- **Not reacting with anger when you hear that they are faring well.**
- **Not getting smug satisfaction when you hear they are not faring well.**
- **Letting it go.**

Despite the prevailing assumption that the other person benefits from your forgiveness, you are actually the one who benefits. You let go of the anger, resentment, pride, and sometimes depression and anxiety.

Depression has been called anger turned inward. When you feel that you can't lash out at the person, you turn the anger in on yourself. Similarly, non-forgiveness can result in anxiety when you feel that you would like to hurt the person and fear your own instincts. Depression, anxiety, and anger all strain your nerves and every system in your body. Consequently, forgiving is good for your health and happiness. Let's get to it!

Exercise 8C—Forgive the Bullies

You will need a pen and your journal, or your Word document. You will also need the pictures and school memorabilia you have used in other exercises.

1. **Remember an incident when you were being bullied. You can use the same one you used in Exercise 8A or 8B, or a different one. If you have a memory of being bullied in adult life, you can use that too. Decide if the incident matters to you now. Is it currently affecting your life?**

2. **If the incident is not currently affecting your life, think of the bully. Can you see him or her or them as having an undeveloped mind, having their own personal problems, or having character flaws? If you are using an adult memory of bullying, keep in mind that some bully's minds never fully develop.**

3. **Decide if you want anything from the person in the way of restitution.**

4. **After answering the questions in Steps 2, and 3, do you still feel anger, sadness, or anxiety about the offense? If no, then you have forgiven.**

5. **If you do feel that the incident is affecting your life, write about how. Remember that journaling has the effect of getting your thoughts out of your head.**

6. **Ask yourself if there is anything you can learn from the incident that occurred.**

7. **When you have completed all these steps, ask yourself if you still have any unwanted feelings about the person and the incident. Ask yourself how you want to feel. Remember that you forgive for yourself, not for the other person. Is the ex-bully (or if it is a current bully) worth your unhappiness now? Forgive because you want to feel good!**

After you forgive someone, you might have to remind yourself that you forgave them. The incident might resurface in your head and elicit anger or sadness as you have been habituated to the grudge. However, if you remind yourself that you forgave, read your journal and remember doing the exercise, you will persist in your forgiveness.

I am excited for you that you now have the tools to move on from past bullying. Before the Columbine High School shooting in 1999, not much attention was paid to bullying and its effects. Columbine increased awareness, and now Kate and many others are helping the cause to stop bullying in schools. I realize that many of you reading this went to school when you were supposed to just handle it yourselves. Now you can put the bullying where it belongs—in the past!

While this chapter has thus far focused on victims of bullying, I imagine that some readers will have been on the other side of the situation at least once in their life, even if it was just in the form of retaliation like Kate tried in middle school. Are there times in your life where maybe you hurt someone else and now you feel guilty wondering if you scarred them for life?

Bryant spent his early years in Freehold, New Jersey. His parents separated while he was a year old, they were never married. He moved to Waretown, New Jersey with his father.

Bryant seemed to have a lot of anger by the time he started school. He was one of the biggest kids in the school and he excelled in sports in elementary school and high school. **Perhaps the anger that he felt during his early years coupled with his size made him bully everyone. He was constantly making fun of his schoolmates and calling them names. Often the school jock will bully kids who are not athletic. Bryant played baseball, basketball, football, and wrestled. However, most of the bullying he did was not physical. He was in occasional fights, but most of the time he verbally abused kids.**

In his sophomore year in high school, Bryant faced a series of tragedies. His father died the summer before sophomore year. Sometime after, the aortic section of Bryant's heart erupted and he had to have open heart surgery to shorten his aortic valve.

The combination of these events would make most people aware of their own mortality. However, Bryant also faced the suicides of a teacher and an ex-girlfriend, a friend that he played football with was killed in a house fire, and a basketball teammate was riding an ATV on the Garden State Parkway and was struck by a car, it was fatal.

Instead of going into despair and committing suicide, Bryant used these tragedies to help others and to make his life more meaningful.

Since he already knew how to bully other people and why bullying happens, he looked for ways to reach out to bullies and encourage them to stop bullying. First he joined the peer leaders, a group of select students at his school who had leadership potential and would use that potential to counsel other students. He spoke to the kids about bullying, study skills, and other issues that school aged children face. The group had a Safe Night at a middle school in the area where Bryant led a group of ten students to create a plan to combat bullying. They created and filmed an anti-bullying video to show in their classrooms.

Bryant recently graduated from college and is studying for his Masters in School Counseling. He did an internship with his grade school where he made a presentation about self-image during National Bullying Prevention Month.

I asked Bryant how he now feels about having bullied so many kids at school. He shared that he is indifferent. This means that he is not proud but he is not plaguing himself with guilt either. This is a healthy attitude for anyone who knows they may have hurt others in the past but now recognize the wrongfulness of it. I define guilt as the emotion someone

feels when they have violated their ethics or have done something bad when they think they are a good person. However, you can still think of yourself as a good person without plaguing yourself with guilt.

Ironically, guilt does not usually prevent the bearer from repeating the offense. When you feel guilt you are giving the offense that you did a lot of thought and emotion and it actually makes you repeat the action because you are so focused on it. It is better to just remind yourself that you are sorry for what you did and let the guilt go.

Bryant has done that and does not feel that he owes anything to the now young adults that he bullied in school. He does not have to find them and invite them to the local bar and buy them a round of drinks. Instead, he uses his experience as a tool to help others.

Earlier in this chapter, we did some exercises to help you if you were the victim of bullying. If you ever were on the other side as someone who may have hurt another person and are now feeling guilty about your behavior, the following exercise should give you some perspective.

Exercise 8D—Do You Mean I Did Not Ruin Anyone for Life?

For this exercise, I highly recommend that you have completed all of the previous exercises in the book, especially the ones about changing your beliefs. You will need a pen and your journal, or your Word document.

1. Consider adopting the following beliefs:

   - People are resilient and can recover from bad experiences.
   - I was immature and the people I bullied probably understand that now.
   - The experience could have made them stronger.
   - If I encounter my former victims, I can and will treat them respectfully.
   - I can teach my own kids how to handle bullying.

2. If you have a profile on Facebook or any of the other social networks, request the friendship of people you may have hurt. You do not have to address the past unless they do. Just express your apologies if they do bring it up. If they do not address the past, just be friendly with them now.

3. If they resist your friendship, or you talk to them and they still seem to be angry with you, forgive yourself. How can you forgive yourself? First, remind yourself that you would not do anything to hurt them now, and remember that people are ultimately responsible for healing themselves. This book, counselors, other self-improvement books and seminars, and the church, among others are there to help them.

When you beat yourself up with guilt and remorse, you are bullying yourself, and if you are replaying your

past negative memories and you are still feeling the bad feelings, you are also bullying yourself. This book is about letting go.

Bullying is not the only trauma that people go through. The next chapter contains stories and exercises showing what to do if you had a life changing tragedy.

CHAPTER 9

Making the Most of Life Changing Tragedies

Kit was a world class juggler. He began juggling and riding the unicycle when he was fourteen years old. He rode in parades in the San Diego area and juggled at carnivals and at the San Diego Zoo. When he was sixteen, he won three hundred dollars on *The Gong Show,* a 1970s equivalent of today's reality shows.

After his win on *The Gong Show,* he went to Hawaii and performed an act with Barrett Feckler, a former basketball player for the Harlem Globetrotters. By this time, he had decided that he was going to make a career of juggling. Determined to be the best in the business, he went to Europe in 1978 to learn from the masters. Like most stars, he had to work his way up the ranks.

After several months of advanced training in Europe, he took his skills to Florida where he became a juggling instructor for the Ringling Brothers Barnum and Bailey Circus Clown College. He enjoyed teaching clowns and continued to do shows at carnivals. This was 1979. After that summer, he and his wife returned to San Diego. Kit was able to juggle six pins at once and was trying for the world record of seven.

At about this time, Kit's wife was looking to relocate to the Philadelphia area of Pennsylvania where her family lived. Kit began looking for acts on the East Coast. In 1981, he got his big break. Bally's Casino in Atlantic City, New Jersey hired him to do a twelve minute juggling act twice a night. Kit was on top of the world. He had a job that was his dream. He worked only twenty-four minutes a night and he loved every minute of it. He had a wife, two young daughters, and the chance to become the greatest juggler in the world.

On Saturday, April 3, 1982 there was a monsoon of a rain storm in Atlantic City. Throughout the day and into the evening, the sky released buckets and buckets of rain that was tossed around in terrible gusts of wind that grew worse with each passing hour. Kit had gone to Bally's in the afternoon for his usual practice, but then returned home to rest before his evening performances. By the time he drove back to the casino in the evening, the rain was even worse. Visibility was near zero. Kit parked in his usual space, unfolded his umbrella and began walking to work. The wind was howling making it difficult to hold the umbrella as he walked towards the casino.

Suddenly a truck appeared from around the corner. Despite having the headlights on, the driver did not see Kit walking across the street and crashed directly into him. Kit was thrown up into the air and landed through the windshield of the truck, shattering the glass. His arm also shattered the side view mirror. He was thrown on the curb where his body finally rested about twenty feet away from the truck.

Thirty seven days later, Kit regained consciousness. He was barely able to move, he was confused, and he was having daily black outs of time. He knew he had been in an accident and was injured. He was depressed and thought of suicide at times. However, these were passing thoughts which he did not allow to take root. He determined to start his life over again, and any thoughts of suicide were eclipsed by thoughts of returning to his life and juggling.

Kit's recovery included relearning to do everything he once did with ease, including such basic functions as walking and talking. As he relearned these skills, he could felt as if his mind and his body were disconnected. He was unable to pronounce certain words, standing was difficult at first, and walking only came after a few months.

After six months, Kit was released from physical therapy. Determined to rebuild his life, he began practicing juggling. At first, he struggled to juggle, dropping juggling balls regularly. During one practice session, one of the balls landed on his head at the same place where he had sustained his injury in the accident. He realized that he would never be the same juggler that he had been. However, he received a lot of support from his family and friends. Eventually he stopped performance juggling and started a salsa business. He continued to give juggling lessons.

From his experiences, **Kit learned that each incident one goes through contains a lesson to be learned such that next time, one can do better.** Years later, he had a series of trials that tested his ability to use this lesson. His wife left him and took his daughters with her. Although Kit realized that the marriage had not been good for a few years, it understandably still devastated him.

A few months later, he was riding his bike, an activity he could still do and enjoyed, when another truck hit him and broke both of his legs. This was actually the third time he had been hit in a span of twenty-eight years and five days. He had always been a good runner. Now he could no longer run. A few months after that, he spent a month in jail for a crime he did not commit.

Kit is a great example of how people can keep their enthusiasm and zest for life despite trials. Today, Kit is a happy man in his fifties who still makes and sells salsa, gives juggling lessons, and writes books on juggling and self-help.

You can learn the same two lessons that Kit learned by following his example. The first and most important life lesson he learned is that you can turn everything that seems like a tragedy in your life into an opportunity. The other lesson, which I think can be applied to any trauma in your life, is to become more compassionate and empathetic towards others who are going through trials.

Example 11—Some Setbacks That Could Become Opportunities

You may still be weighed down by the effects of memories where the following events happened. This is just a partial list.

- **The loss of your job.**
- **Not getting a job you want.**
- **The loss of your marriage.**
- **Not getting the romantic partner you want.**
- **A physical injury.**
- **Having been bullied at school or work.**
- **Having been abused by parents.**
- **Conviction of a crime.**
- **Not making the team.**
- **Not making the school show.**
- **Not making the first chair in the band.**
- **Not getting a promotion because someone younger or better looking was promoted.**
- **Doing some work online that you are proud of and someone hacked it.**
- **A serious illness that has left you unable to work or to do activities you used to enjoy.**

If any of these things have happened to you and you still have feelings about it, then try the next exercise.

Exercise 9A—Turn a Setback into an Opportunity

Do this exercise in a quiet place where you will not be disturbed. You will need a pen and your journal, or your Word document.

1. Think of an incident in your life that seemed traumatic and took a long time to get over. If it is an incident that you still feel traumatized about, use it.

2. Write the details of the incident as you remember them. If this gets too intense, take a five minute break, do something relaxing or enjoyable such as listening to your MP3 player or playing a short video game. When you return, don't write anything else about the incident. You have done enough to get in touch with the feelings.

3. Think of the beliefs you have formed from the memory. For example, if the memory is of a recent job loss, the belief may be that you will never work in that field again. If it is of a disabling injury, you may be thinking that you will never gain your capabilities back.

4. Think of anyone you know who may have had a similar challenge in their life. How did they deal with it?

5. If you don't know anyone who had a similar challenge, or only know people who let that challenge ruin their lives, then ask yourself if you could overcome it.

6. **Ask yourself if there is anything you can learn from the experience.**

7. **Say the phrase, "I am glad that _____ happened because I learned _____."**

Do you now feel differently about the memory as compared to when we started this exercise? If you do, then you could use this exercise for any memory that you still have negative feelings about. If you were unable to find a positive, then here are some examples of how the situations in Example 11 might be seen as a positive.

Example 12—Redefine the Setbacks as Opportunities

- **The loss of your job—time to redefine who you are and enjoy some free time.**
- **Not getting the job you want—decide that there is a better job for you (useful assumption).**
- **The loss of your marriage—time to do new things while appreciating what you had.**
- **Not getting the romantic partner you want—there is somebody better waiting for you.**
- **A physical injury—redefine your life as Kit and Nancy did (you will read about Nancy next).**
- **Having been bullied at school or work—help others who were bullied or are being bullied as Kate and Bryant do.**

- **Having been abused by parents—be a better parent to your kids. Define yourself independent of what your parents' treatment of you was.**
- **Having been convicted of a crime—start over despite the odds.**
- **Not making the team—try another sport or a different activity.**
- **Someone was unfairly promoted over you—redefine who you are independent of work.**
- **Doing some work online and someone hacked it—learn some new laws associated with internet piracy and hacking. It is also an opportunity to learn perseverance—if you are creative enough, you will create more works and protect them.**
- **A physical injury that left you unemployable and unable to do the physical activities you used to enjoy—learn from Kit that you can learn and enjoy activities different from what you used to do and that you can still be successful.**

One of the ways that disappointments and setbacks become opportunities is that they make you more compassionate than you might have been otherwise. Many people who work as counselors, social workers, and teachers went through family dysfunction, bullying, and other things that made them compassionate and that made them want to help people.

I remember that one of my graduate professors told us that counselors were unlikely to have been the captain of the football team or the homecoming queen when they were in school. Most people who are compassionate enough to be a counselor probably experienced rejection in their lives and that experience made them empathetic.

I can imagine some of you are thinking, I am compassionate and I had a good life. I am not saying that being rejected and experiencing trauma are the only ways to develop a caring attitude, but they are great experiences to use to make the most out of past hurts.

Nancy is a sixty-two year old Trauma Recovery Expert/ Disability Life Coach. In 1971, she was a twenty year old undergraduate student at the University of Michigan. She was a good student and sorority president with a rebellious streak. She describes herself as a hippie who wore clean clothes. Nancy believed that she had her life completely planned. She was well organized and good at multitasking long before it became fashionable.

One cold November day, on her way home from student teaching, Nancy was a passenger in a car accident and sustained a severe head injury. She was in a coma for two and a half months. When she began to regain consciousness, she refused to acknowledge that she had new limitations. Although she had problems, she would find another way.

Less than one year after her injury, Nancy returned to college. She was able to earn a Bachelor of Science, but was unable to do her fieldwork in a classroom. Multitasking was no longer her forte, so she could not keep pace with the multiplicity of demands in an elementary school classroom.

One year later, Nancy attended graduate school at the University of Wisconsin-Madison. She earned her Master of Social Work because as she says, she was good at going to school. After graduate school, she moved away from home, but had trouble living on her own. It would be fourteen years, 1985, before Nancy would realize that she couldn't do everything that she wanted to do.

Now more than forty years after the injury, Nancy still does not recall much of the first few months that she was awake after the accident. Similar to Kit, she had to relearn everything—how to walk, how to talk, and even how to take care of her most basic needs. In her early efforts to talk, Nancy would pause for several seconds between words and sentences. People called her unflattering names, as the term developmentally disabled was not used in 1972.

Today, Nancy is a Disability Life Coach. She functions as a Trauma Recovery Expert and specializes in assisting survivors of trauma to reintegrate into an active and interdependent life. She has a husband who supports and assists her in doing what she can no longer do for herself. She struggles with fatigue, organization, finances, and she has memory problems. Nancy views her head injury as the enemy that she has to battle on a daily basis. Her life experiences make her understanding and empathetic towards survivors and clients and caregivers, That's what makes her an effective Disability Life Coach.

Although you may not have gone through what Kit and Nancy experienced, you probably have had some experiences that made you empathetic. Let's find out.

Exercise 9B—Do You Empathize?

For this exercise, you will need a pen and your journal, or your Word document.

1. **Take the memory that you used for Exercise 9A or a different unpleasant memory, maybe something you used for an exercise in a previous chapter.**
2. **Imagine someone else going through the same thing you went through within the memory.**
3. **Notice how you feel about that person.**
4. **If you feel how that person must feel, you know how to be empathetic.**
5. **If you did not feel empathetic, perhaps you are in denial that you went through the experience. If you feel inclined, imagine yourself back in the situation standing next to the other person. Notice if you feel empathetic now.**
6. **Finish this sentence: I learned from this exercise that _____.**
7. **Finish this sentence: I can now understand people who go through _____.**

As you did this exercise, were you aware of the idea that when you go through a difficult time, you are able to feel for others who have gone through the same thing? When I was in junior high and early high school, I was very self-absorbed. Some of my schoolmates accused me of being conceited because I was so smart. I believe that one of the reasons I decided to go into the counseling field was to get out of myself and to start caring about other people. It felt very good to care about others and to help them.

You may have discovered something similar when you did this exercise. If you did not increase your empathy skills, maybe it would help you to volunteer somewhere, such as a soup kitchen or your local hospital. It feels good to focus on others in a caring way. You may be wondering why you need to be empathetic. It can teach you people skills which you need for most jobs.

As the author of this book, I have done all of the exercises that I created and listed in this book. However, this next one was the hardest for me to do. It is about accepting your limitations.

My wife and family can tell you that the only thing that I will admit that I am not good at is admitting that I am not good at things. Nancy, who you read about, is a great example of a person who can accept their limitations but keeps striving to improve herself. Try Exercise 9C and see how you fare.

Exercise 9C—Accepting Your Limitations

You will need a pen and your journal, or your Word document. Reviewing your answers to Exercise 7 may be helpful here.

1. **Review the weaknesses that you had during your school years from Exercise 7. Ask yourself, has anything changed as far as what I think my strengths and weaknesses are now?**
2. **If you are an adult, look at the past few years and what you have done well and not so well.**
3. **Ask yourself, do I have enough strengths that I can use such that the weaknesses don't matter?**
4. **If your answer to number 3 was yes, you have a good perspective on yourself, congratulations!**
5. **If your answer was no, ask yourself, is there any one thing that I have that I can use? Go back over previous exercises and see if there is something you may have forgotten about. Ask family or friends who are supportive.**

When you think about it, who would really want to be good at everything? You would have so much pressure in life and no free time to relax. Here are some useful beliefs to adopt about perfection.

Example 13—I Don't Want to Be Perfect

- **Nobody would want to be around a perfect person because they would feel diminished.**
- **Being perfect would be too much pressure. You would always be afraid of making a mistake.**
- **People would expect too much from you.**
- **You would always be under the microscope.**
- **You could never laugh at yourself because you would never make mistakes to laugh about.**

After reading this, I hope you can see that your limitations can serve you. They can provide you with as much direction as your strengths, and they can guide you in what not to pursue. They can also give you a way to laugh at yourself. Finally, when you fail at something or lose your ability to do something, your limitations can make you more compassionate.

In the next chapter, we are going to look at specific area of your life that might need some healing in order for you to move forward in your life. The next topic is one that many people see as being responsible for their present ills.

CHAPTER 10

Give Yourself and Your Parents a Break

Job Description—This job generally lasts from eighteen to thirty years. You will start out in the hospital where you will be given a miniature person that makes loud sounds, has bad plumbing and needs frequent cleaning, and will tend to keep you up throughout the night.

Over the course of the eighteen to thirty years that you will perform this job, this miniature person will grow and get older and continue to cost you more and more money and time. You will have to routinely purchase new clothing and toys, as well as copious amounts of food. In the earlier years, you will also have to dress and feed this miniature person several times every day. Somewhere around half way to the eighteen to thirty years, maybe in year ten or twelve, you will find that this job also requires you to become a taxi driver. At times, you may feel you need a pair of pliers to remove yourself from the steering wheel of your car.

If you wind up having more than one of these miniature people as your very own, you may need to combine the skills and duties of an attorney, judge, and labor mediator.

When these people start playing outside, you will need to be an emergency medical technician and a nurse. When they enter high school, you may need to be a career counselor and birth control counselor. At the same time that you are juggling all of these skills, you may find yourself being accused of not knowing anything. This miniature person who has now grown to be two inches taller than you, however, knows everything and will make sure that you also know that they know everything.

Even once these people are grown, the job may not be over. You may need to be a marriage counselor and financial advisor. You have already been an accountant for many years.

What are the benefits of this job? Well there are no financial benefits, but over the course of the time described, you may have to pay a quarter of a million dollars to get to do the job. You also must be careful that over all those years, you never make a mistake because if you do, the job comes with the following guarantee: if anything is not perfect in the lives of these now grown people, you will receive one hundred percent of the blame.

Perhaps you are wondering who would want this job. The statistics show that most people in the history of the world have taken on the challenge of being a parent. Although some do it reluctantly, most parents do the job voluntarily. Although I feel that the counseling profession does a lot of good, it has caused parents to be the scapegoat of every dysfunctional person in the world. Parents get blamed for everything. Some will say the reason their own marriage failed is because their parents were divorced. Other will say they didn't get a good job because careers were not emphasized in their homes while growing up. Some will blame their shyness on the fact that their father yelled at them all the time. Others will say they are obese because their parents didn't teach them that physical activity was important or because their mother never cooked and now they don't know how to make healthy food.

Some parent blamers go deeper. If they can't keep a job and are afraid of authority figures, they blame their parents for being too critical when they were growing up. If they are having trouble parenting their own children, they blame their parents for not being good. Some people who had critical parents vow to never raise their voice or criticize their children, but then they spoil them. The list can go on and on.

When I worked in the psychiatric hospital, one of the doctors and his wife had raised several children. **They told me that when their children turned eighteen, they told them they were now on their own and could make their lives whatever they wanted. This sounds incredibly freeing. The premise of this book is that you can free yourself from the effects of your past negative memories.**

It is useful to replace a memory of something unpleasant with something more pleasant. However, humorous memories give you an added edge. Laughter is the quickest way to get out of a bad feeling.

Perhaps you are now thinking to yourself, Yes, but I have some bad family memories and I don't have your memory, Healy. You may not remember every day or every incident, but you do remember good and bad events. I have one word of caution here. If your family memories include physical, emotional, or sexual abuse from other family members, it would help you to see a therapist in addition to doing this exercise.

Exercise 10—My Family Was Amazing

You will need a pen and your journal, or your Word document and some old pictures.

1. **Go through your previous entries and find any memories of your parents and family.**
2. **Make a numbered list of the positive memories. Make another numbered list of the negative memories of your parents.**
3. **Pick a positive memory and write down everything you remember about it. Don't rush through this. As you write the details, stop and dwell on them. Repeat this exercise with another positive memory.**
4. **Now repeat Step 3 with a negative memory of parents. However, rush through this step and do not dwell on the negative too long.**
5. **Repeat Step 3 with the same positive memory or a different one.**

How do you feel about your parents now? Hopefully you are able to minimize the bad memory. You can repeat this exercise with any negative memory, and you can simplify the exercise by using the same positive memory each time you go through the exercise in combination with different negative memories. This may be necessary if you feel that you have more negative than positive memories. Or, it may be that you have more positive memories with one parent than with another. You can be grateful for the parent that you have lots of good memories about and hopefully retrieve at least one positive memory of the other parent.

How can you make your seemingly negative memories of parents amazing? The best way is to see if there is learning in the memory. Everything that you have ever experienced can be an opportunity to learn.

Example 14—My Parents Taught Me (Hypothetical)

- **They never taught me anything. Lesson: I learned to be self-sufficient and seek others who will teach me things.**
- **They yelled at me and never let me express myself. Lesson: I don't have to have that kind of person in my life now. I can express myself.**
- **They used me as a scapegoat. Lesson: I can earn and demand respect and avoid people who don't respect me now.**

- **They favored my charming brother or sister. Lesson: I can prefer the company of people who enjoy me and who I enjoy being with.**
- **They never took an interest in my development. Lesson: I can achieve things now and find supportive people in my life.**
- **They wanted me to be a piece of clay that they molded and they didn't care about what I wanted. Lesson: I can be who I am now.**

These are just a few examples of how parents can be disappointing. My recommendation if you are still blaming your parents for things is to go to the exercises in Chapter 8. If you feel that parents bullied you, then do Exercise 8A and 8B. If they disappointed you in other ways, then do Exercise 8C to forgive them.

What if you were raised in a horribly dysfunctional environment and you could not think of any good memories? The good news is that you can still recover. The next chapter will give you a few more techniques to help free you from your past.

CHAPTER 11

Break the Rules

On Sunday, September 3, 1939 there was massive chaos in London and all over Europe. The news came out that Hitler had just invaded Poland. News of war is particularly scary for children. They imagine all kinds of ways that their safety could be threatened, including that the war could come right to their house and they could be killed in a bombing or other incident. The best thing that you can do to comfort a child is to reassure them that the family will stick together and try to make their lives as routine and predictable as possible.

Yvonne was just twelve days short of her sixth birthday when the news of Hitler came. She and her family had been on vacation and were making preparations to go back home to London. Yvonne knew something was wrong though as they weren't making any preparations for her to go back home with them. She asked where everyone was going, and what was going to happen to her since they were leaving her behind, but they gave her no answer.

In war torn Britain, it was common practice for families to leave their small children after which the government would find foster parents for them with no qualifications other than they have an available room in their home. After being left by her family the first time 1939, Yvonne began having nightmares. She described the following six months as ghastly. She stayed with an elderly couple and their grandson. The grandmother did well in taking care of Yvonne's basic physical needs but she didn't have much to do with Yvonne beyond that. The grandfather was kind to Yvonne and so she especially adored him. The grandson was in the Royal Air Force and was not home often because of his duties.

By the time the war ended, Yvonne had been abandoned by her family three times. The third time was near Oxford where she had caretakers who did not speak to her for nearly a year.

School was difficult for Yvonne. By age eight, she had experienced so much hurt and abandonment that she would not get close to anyone. She never made friends in school. She was a good kid who was helpful, but she never cultivated friendships. Her situation was similar to children in military families. They grow up expecting to change schools and be in different parts of the country at different times, so they often do not make friends. Yvonne not only attended different schools, but was also in different households.

Things were not much better when Yvonne was at home with her family after the war ended. Her family had a lot of secrets, and I am not talking about the ingredients in mom's amazing breakfast muffins that she refused to reveal to anyone. Many families would keep secrets from select members as well as from society as a whole. The rules of modesty in that day dictated that family affairs were not to leave the walls of one's home. On Yvonne's twenty-first birthday, the man who she thought was her father revealed to her that he was not her real father. Her mother cried. Later Yvonne discovered that everyone else in the family knew, including cousins who were younger than her. Yvonne was the family secret!

Among other rules, Yvonne was not permitted to complain. When Yvonne was fifteen years old, she was in the throes of teenage anguish. Acne covered her face and entire body. As most teenagers would see this as the end of the world, when she complained about it, her aunt would say, "Pull yourself together, you have a rich girl's complaint." Years later, Yvonne's mother died while Yvonne was pregnant. Her aunt chastised her for crying, telling her, "Don't cry, it will hurt the baby." Ironically, alcohol was allowed during pregnancy, but crying at funerals wasn't.

Yvonne's life did not improve when she married. Years of invalidation by her family taught her that others' wants and needs were more important than her own. Yvonne's husband was a womanizer, and she allowed him to do whatever he wanted without question. She believed that she was never to question anyone's wants or needs. She was there to take care of him regardless of how he treated her. He not only cheated on her but also subjected her to constant emotional and psychological abuse. The abuse took the form of the silent treatment, which was similar to what she endured with her family of origin and her foster families.

In 1968, at age thirty-five and with four young children, Yvonne's husband convinced her that there was a better life for them in the United States. On Monday, October 28, they arrived in Philadelphia. Yvonne was severely depressed and started therapy.

After three years of therapy, Yvonne had a significant turning point in her life. For the first time in her life, she asserted herself. One day, she told her husband that she no longer wanted to be with him. She proudly describes this as the beginning of her recovery.

Many people think of recovery as being limited to drugs and alcohol. However, there are many ways to recover. You can recover from overeating, biting your nails, chocolate addiction, among other things. For Yvonne, she needed to recover from codependency.

Codependents are people who have no sense of self-worth outside of taking care of others. They have no self-respect and they tolerate abuse from others because they need to take care of the other person. If there is no one there to take care of regardless of how that other person treats them, the codependent has no reason to live.

After asserting herself to her husband, Yvonne was convinced that therapy really works, and she decided to go to school to be a grief counselor. She started a practice, and found that she related to her clients so strongly that she should continue her own therapy.

First she went to a program called Adult Children of Alcoholics. She understood and related to all of the concepts. She learned that she was a person in her own right. All of her wants and needs count. She was allowed to experience her feelings and vent them to trusted people. Slowly but surely she let go of the dysfunctional rules she was raised with. She could laugh, she could cry, she could get angry, she could express when she did not like something, and she could ask for what she wanted.

Sometime after her divorce, Yvonne met a man named John. He was the most normal man in Yvonne's world. His credentials included that he was a gentleman, that he treated Yvonne with respect, that he showed up for dates when he said he would, that he wanted Yvonne exclusively, and that he had no problems with alcohol.

Yvonne had mixed feelings about this man. After a lifetime of learning not to trust anyone, she put him to the test. Fortunately, another one of John's qualities was patience. Now after more than twenty-five years, they are still together.

I first met Yvonne on Monday, December 17, 1990. I was working in a psychiatric hospital while enduring my final year of graduate school. She wanted to form an agency entitled Connections for Living. It included support groups for people who were overcoming the effects of dysfunctional memories. I could have run one of the groups but when Yvonne learned of my memory, she commissioned me to teach a memory improvement course instead.

By the time I knew Yvonne, she was a happy and dynamic fifty-seven year old woman. She has a great sense of humor and is very playful. Yvonne's slogan was and still is, "Have the kind of day you want." When life becomes challenging, she tells herself, "I am not going to let this beat me."

As an adult, Yvonne still has flashbacks of her childhood traumas. On Wednesday, January 16, 1991 she was driving to the hospital to conduct a seminar when she heard on the radio that the United States had invaded Baghdad. Yvonne started crying in the car and yelled, "You are not going to get my sons!"

A trigger is when you encounter something that triggers a flashback to a traumatic memory. Understandably, Yvonne was triggered by news of the war and was having an emotional flashback to that day when she was six years old and World War II had begun. The news made her think that her sons might have to go to Iraq where they would be killed in battle. She conducted her seminar that night but needed a lot of emotional support from her significant other, John, her friends, and her family. September 11, 2001 was difficult for her for the same reasons.

Despite the flashbacks, Yvonne recovered quickly. She now had coping tools that she did not have as a child. She knew that she was now an adult who could take care of her inner child and that she had developed relationships with people who cared about her and would support her.

As Yvonne was recovering from her dysfunctional upbringing, she identified a bunch of dysfunctional rules that she was living by. Yvonne realized these rules were working against her and needed to be revised. Here are some examples of unwritten rules that many people live by perhaps without even realizing it. Please note that this list comes from my years of working with troubled people. They are not necessarily Yvonne's rules.

Example 15—Rules for Living That You Can Revise

- I must never cry in front of other people.
- I must hide my feelings because real men are strong and don't feel.
- My idea of a good vacation is that we drive six hundred miles to our destination in a non-air conditioned car with the kids' MP3 blaring and of course, I do all the driving. What everyone wants is more important than what I want.
- If the kids and my spouse are happy, I am happy. If they are sad, I am sad. I don't have feelings of my own.
- If I just worked for sixteen hours, eight of which included a graveyard shift, and I come home on Saturday morning to my kids demanding to go bowling, I take them.
- I perform a great service because I build everyone's ego. When a boss that bullied me and fired me

sidelined my career and bad mouthed me to the unemployment office, the most important thing was to acknowledge that the boss meant well and is a terrific person.

- I always say yes when a friend asks me to go out.
- I always say yes when my job asks me to work overtime even when I don't need the money and am tired. (I know what you're thinking, who in the world does not need extra money?)
- When I am in meetings at work, I never express any ideas of how to improve things because I think I will be reprimanded for rocking the boat.

Then there is the wonderful world of relationships.

- You must be willing to drink too much, flirt with the opposite sex constantly, and lie about everything.
- If you have held a steady job for a year or more, don't even think we will go out.
- The same rule applies if you are a responsible single parent and love your kids. I am afraid you will love me too much.
- You must give me a reason for living. This could include picking you up off the floor when you have passed out in a drunken stupor.
- Call me all kinds of creative names and accuse me of things. I will build you up as the greatest person who ever lived. I know you mean well!

Hopefully you now have some ideas of rules you are living by that are holding you back in life. Maybe you related to some of the ideas in this example, or maybe you thought of your own. Exercise 11A will give you a chance to explore your unwritten rules and help you to revise them.

Exercise 11A—Be a Rebel and Break the Rules

As always, you will need a pen and your journal, or your Word document. Plan to carry it with you for a day or two.

1. **For the next day or two, record any thoughts you have and actions you take that seem annoying or do not serve you.**
2. **When you have compiled a list, it could be one or two things, or it could be twenty or more rules that don't serve you. Use the previous example for ideas. Write a contradiction to the rule. For example, "I can laugh," "I can say no to my kids when I don't feel up to meeting the demand."**
3. **It may feel strange or funny to declare your new freedom, but repeat it as many times as it takes for you to feel okay about it.**
4. **Get in a relaxed state and visualize yourself practicing your new freedom (let's call it new freedom instead of a new rule). It may be that you visualize taking a lunch break at work if you do not normally do so. It may be that you visualize**

telling your kids that they can go bowling tomorrow. Imagining this in a relaxed state can help you be comfortable and dissolve guilt, and it can transfer to the real situation.

5. **When you have the opportunity, practice your new freedom in a situation.**

6. **Take a few pages of your journal or your Word document and write at the top of a new page, My Declaration of Independence. Whenever you think of a rule that does not serve you, write a statement of your freedom that contradicts that rule.**

Now that you have completed Exercise 11A, you have learned a new way to get rid of all your rules that are holding you back in life. Please feel free to return to this exercise repeatedly as you find yourself acting on or thinking about your old rules. If you find yourself slipping back into the old patterns, just look at your journal and remind yourself that you don't have to repeat the pattern. Beating yourself up for mistakes is also a good rule to break!

When you find that you have nothing left to perfect, congratulations, you are free and independent!

Remember that some rules that you were taught are good for you. When my father taught me how to mow the lawn, he said to wear your hardest shoes for safety reasons. Now, forty-two years later, I still wear my steel tipped work boots when I mow the lawn. My mother taught me to work as if everything depended on me and pray as if everything depended on God. Many of you have memories of being taught good rules.

Most of us have rules about when to be happy, sad, and angry. We were taught to be happy on vacation, when we accomplish something, and when it is sunny out. We were taught to be sad when things do not happen the way we like, or at a funeral.

On Friday, December 10, 1976 I was at my grandfather's viewing. He was a wonderful man and everyone liked him. So many people came to the viewing, it seemed as if the line to his coffin would never end.

I decided to sit down and wait until the line was shorter before going up myself. As I sat and watched the procession, my Aunt Lee and Uncle Frank came in and sat down in the chairs next to me. Instead of saying hello, my uncle greeted me by saying, "I see you got a haircut. You were starting to look like a bear." I shook my head and pursed my lips in an effort not to laugh and be disrespectful at a wake. Then he nudged me and started laughing. Finally, I gave in and started laughing, too.

Being a deep thinking person that, I decided that it was okay to laugh at a funeral. My uncle was a funny man who frequently makes sad people laugh. Grandpa was a loving man who would have wanted to be remembered happily rather than being mourned.

If laughter can be appropriate at a funeral, it can be appropriate anywhere. Here is an important question to ask, **do you know anyone who cannot laugh but still wants to go on living?**

Yvonne's sense of humor was one of the best of anyone I have known. When I attended her seminars, she often referred to herself as "That English woman." She is spontaneous and playful—pretty good for someone who had such a traumatic childhood.

Example 16—Serious Ways to Develop a Serious Sense of Humor

- **Notice other people's quirks.**
- **Notice and accept your own quirks.**
- **Remember Example 13—you really don't want to be perfect.**
- **Laugh at how serious some people are.**
- **Think of some ineffective stress management techniques. For example, Sean, who you will read about later, is someone I know who told me about how he relieves stress by bouncing a giant ball, but bouncing the ball would stress out his roommate. I thought that was funny.**
- **You can also use humor to build your own self esteem. When Kate told me that she gets through to the kids because she looks like a twelve year old, we both laughed.**
- **Think of multiple uses of words and expressions. One time, I was talking to a teenager who needed**

money so they were working part time in a bakery. I said, "So you are kneading dough because you need dough." It's okay to laugh at the corniness.

- **Remember that something can be funny to you even if others don't see the humor in it. You don't have to be a professional comedian to appreciate humor.**

Please keep in mind that your sense of humor does not come with a license to kill. Naturally you are not going to laugh in your boss's or teacher's face if you think they are being too serious. Nor are you going to make fun of a stranger's quirk. You can amuse yourself but if everyone made fun of everyone's quirks out loud, a lot of people would be offended and fists would be flying.

Exercise 11B—You Can Find Laughter in Your Memories

You will need a pen and your journal, or your Word document. You will be looking through what you've written so far.

1. **Look through all of the memories that you have recorded.**
2. **Randomly pick one of those memories to meditate on. Decide whether or not there is anything humorous about it.**

3. **If you don't think of anything humorous that occurred, is there anything that could have occurred that would have been funny?**
4. **Do this for another memory.**
5. **Decide to see something funny in your experiences at least once a day.**

Now that you have completed this chapter, you have more tools at your disposal to heal past hurts. You can stop following rules that don't serve you, and you can lighten up! Carpe Diem—Seize the Day! The next chapter will show you how to identify areas of your life where you might be stuck and how to overcome those obstacles.

CHAPTER 12

Please Rescue Me, I Am Stuck Repeating the Past

When I participated in the memory study at the University of California, I asked for the names and numbers of the other subjects that they studied who have the same ability that I have. They emailed everyone and out of the other eleven, six of them consented to contact me.

Sean, from Annapolis, Maryland was the subject who showed the most interest. Since 2011, we have become good friends. You can only imagine how some of our conversations go. We take turns throwing out dates and compare what we were doing.

For example, on Friday, November 14, 1986 it was very cold where I was. I had started a new job in a security office and the vice president threw a crumbled paper at me to help me "Lighten up." Sean said he went on a high school class trip and rode horses. We can do the same thing for any date since the early '80s when Sean began remembering each day of his life. If you would like to watch a video of the entertaining and unusual conversations we have, go to my website: www.phenomenalmemory.com.

You may recall from Chapter 1 that it took me a long time to learn how to handle the constant memories that kept popping into my head all the time. **Sean has had a particularly hard time with memories of rejection from women. Whenever he starts a new relationship, memories of past rejections fill his mind.**

Sean shared with me some of his memories with women, and he is planning to write his own book on the subject. He allowed me to share one of his memories which was particularly dramatic.

Sean works as a Food and Beverage Director for a Downtown Major East Coast City Theater. It is a demanding job as they feature some of the most popular shows.

On Monday, October 31, 2005, Sean was feeling tired and stressed after a busy weekend of sellout crowds at the theater. He needed to unwind. First he went to his apartment and kept bouncing an oversized ball hard against the floor. This had become a regular relaxation technique for Sean despite the fact that it irritated his roommate. Once Sean was feeling more relaxed, he went out for pizza.

While he was in the pizza parlor, a friend, Ray, called and asked if he would like to go to a local bar. Sean is an extrovert. When he is stressed, he goes out with friends, where as an introvert prefers to sit quietly at home in their bathrobe, read, have a glass of warm milk, and then retire. Sean jumped at the opportunity to go to the bar.

Around eight o'clock, they arrived at the bar. Halloween decorations filled the place, and there were people in costumes. People talked excitedly about the start of the hockey season, after being deprived the previous year due to a Player's Union strike.

There was one seat left and in the next seat was a lady reading the newspaper. She had just finished her second drink. Ray introduced them. She responded, "Hi Sean, I'm Lisa." He introduced himself and made a sarcastic remark about her reading a newspaper and drinking at the same time.

Sean ordered his own drink. A friend of his, Debbie, also happened to be at the bar. She approached Sean and explained that she had season tickets for the hockey team. She wanted to give away the tickets for the game later that week. Ray suggested that Sean and Lisa could go together. Sean and Lisa agreed and arranged to meet the before the game in the parking lot of Eve's at five thirty for the seven thirty game.

When Sean arrived at five thirty, Lisa was not there, so he decided to have a beer at the bar while he waited for her. Lisa arrived at five thirty-five, sat down, and ordered another drink. Within minutes, she was finished with that drink and ordered another one while Sean was still working on his first beer.

By quarter of seven, Lisa had finished four drinks. She took Sean's hand and said, "I don't want to go to the game, but I want to go downtown with you."

The couple proceeded downtown where Sean chose another bar for them to hang out. As they walked up the stairs, she asked him a question about if he found her attractive. He answered in the affirmative to which she replied that that was the response she wanted.

When they arrived at the bar, she ordered another drink. He ordered a drink with fried calamari and pizza, as he knew he would be the designated driver. She ate only a little of the calamari and pizza.

It was around eight thirty when Lisa finished her fifth drink and had just ordered a sixth. In her drunkenness, she grabbed Sean's leg and said, "Let's cut to the chase— marry me tomorrow." When Sean said they should get to know each other first, she mocked him saying, "Sean, you are too much of a play it safe guy." She then proceeded to order another drink.

At that point, three of Sean's friends came in. One friend, Laurie, said, "Sean, go home and leave her here. She's a big girl and can get a ride home."

Sean ignored the comment and went into the bathroom. When he came out, Lisa was talking to another man. Lisa eventually came back and started talking to Sean again as she ordered another drink. Sean overheard people saying that he was like a running back that dropped the ball but recovered it, referring to how Lisa walked away for a while to talk to another man, but now was talking to Sean again.

Now intoxicated, Lisa wasn't able to finish her next drink. When she got up to go to the bathroom, Sean noticed that she was staggering. She was in the restroom for a while and the bartender's girlfriend had to eventually bring her out of the bathroom.

Sean finally escorted Lisa out to the car where they started kissing. Somehow, Lisa managed to direct Sean to her house despite being completely intoxicated. Sean walked Lisa into her home and left only once she was settled into bed. Sean finally arrived at his own house around four thirty in the morning. At seven in the morning, he got up, tired and sweating, and went to a meeting in a city an hour away from his home. He overheard some of the other people attending the meeting as they made some smart remarks about his raffled condition. Despite the criticism, Sean continued on with his day.

After such an ordeal, you would think Sean would crash in bed and sleep for about sixteen hours. That was the plan until Brian called him and invited him back to the bar. He told Sean he could have dinner and anything he wanted for free after what he went through the night before with Lisa. When Sean arrived in his apartment, his roommate, who had not been home the night before, teased him about the incident.

Lisa called Sean the next day and thanked him for taking care of her. However, he never heard from her again.

Sean has had many other embarrassing and dramatic incidents with women. He replays the rejections in his head over and over again. Is it surprising that he has no luck with women given that all he can think about is how badly things usually go?

When you replay a bad experience in your head over and over, you increase the chances of something like what you're thinking actually happening because you are conditioning your brain to repeat a similar incident. The only exception to Sean's romantic rejections was when a lady he had dated stalked him for over a year when he tried to get rid of her. Take your pick, which would be worse?

Today, Sean is learning to have more positive relationships with women. He is staying away from the ones who could get him in trouble and learning to think of himself as someone who has success in relationships.

Is there any way that you are stuck repeating the past? You do not have to have Highly Superior Memory to have bad memories flooding your brain and marring your self-confidence. Let's find out by doing Exercise 12.

Exercise 12—Where Are You Stuck?

You will need a pen and your journal, or your Word document. Pick a quiet room and a time where you will not be disturbed for a half hour to an hour.

1. **Think of some area of your life where you remember a lot of negative things. It could be failures in relationships, being told you can't manage money or play golf, or it could be something more general such as being told you will never amount to anything.**

2. **Now think of some area of your life and an incident where you feel that you can't seem to move forward.**

3. **Now, I know you are already an old pro at retrieving memories and visualizing them. This time we will be taking it a step further. Instead of just visualizing the memory, you will be giving it a different outcome.**

4. **Write down the memory as it happened. Then write how you would have liked it to happen.**

5. **Get in a comfortable position. Breathe in and out until you feel totally relaxed. Visualize the incident**

but be creative, think and picture it the way you would like it to be.

6. **Repeat this exercise as often as you need to until you really start believing that you can move forward.**

I can imagine that you might be asking yourself if a visualizing exercise will really make you all of the sudden good at relationships or money or whatever else it is that you might be visualizing. The truth is that first you need to get your confidence right and your belief that you can, then the next step is to do the work. When you condition your brain to believe that you can do it, you will naturally do the work and learn what you need to do.

Sean is learning to make better choices with women now, and he is being selective about women he will date. He has had no incidents like the one with Lisa since he began doing these exercises.

Imagine that you are not good at managing your money. After doing this exercise a few times, you may feel more confident to learn how to manage and invest your money more wisely and responsibly from tutorials on the internet or from books you could buy.

We have now covered many aspects of past memories and how to heal them and yourself. Now it's time to look at the other end of being stuck in the past. What if your memories are so awesome that the present seems dull and depressing?

CHAPTER 13

What to Do If Those Were the Days

Throughout the history of music, there have been songs about the good old days. For the generation who remembers the '60s, there was "Those Were the Days". Then in the '70s, there was the theme song from the sitcom *All in the Family* with the same title. Later in the '70s, there was "The Way We Were" and "The Times of Your Life".

People who enjoy reminiscing go to their class reunions to posture but also to talk about old times. When there isn't a reunion, they spend hours on Facebook pages dedicated to hosting communities of their classes from high school or college. Remember the time you snuck out of class and went to the grand opening of the new McDonald's? I admit I am guilty of this.

Then there are the jokes about the weather. During a 1988 heat wave, I remember reading in the paper, "At least you don't have old people saying 'It don't get hot like it used to.'"

I have emphasized in this book that it is good to recall your positive memories. The past should not consume your present. Reminiscing, however, should not get to the point where you enjoy being in those past memories better than being in your present life.

You may be thinking, Yes, but I hate my life now. I used to have a job, now I am unemployed. I used to be happily married, now I am divorced. This chapter will focus on what you can do if your memories seem better than your life now.

Example 17—Reasons Why Those Were the Days

- **My kids liked me when they were little.**
- **We used to have a bigger house.**
- **I used to be happily married.**
- **I used to be a CEO, now I am a store manager.**
- **I grew up in a big house. We had a shore house and went on great vacations. Now I am an unemployed college graduate.**
- **I used to open and close big businesses, now I am retired and bored with golf. (I hope there is no International Golfers Association that will lobby to ban the sale of this book. Golf is okay, really.)**
- **I used to be good looking, now nobody notices when I walk into a room.**
- **I used to be athletic, now it hurts to bend down and plant flowers.**
- **I used to travel all over the world, now I am in assisted living.**

You get the idea. Maybe you are frustrated in several aspects of life or perhaps in just one aspect of life. Maybe you could not go to your favorite vacation place this year because you did not get a tax refund, but everything else is good.

People have many different wants and needs, and they vary by person and by degree. Ironically, people have a need to feel connected to others, but they also have a need to stand out and be recognized for their achievements. We have a need for excitement and adventure, but also a need for safety, order, and predictability.

Then there is the need to have control over our lives and the need to be accepted. Some people have a strong need to care about others and help them, and others have a need to compete and win. **Wow! God sure has a sense of humor. He created all of these needs that seem to contradict each other.**

As you read the last paragraph, you may have realized that you have stronger needs for certain things that other people may not necessarily even care about. For example, some people have a need to connect with other people while others are perfectly fine spending days at a time alone. Some people don't feel they need to stand out while others always want to be the center of attention. Maybe you are someone who would prefer to have the same office job with minimal travel for thirty years and spend the weekends watching videos with your family. It would be hard for you to understand someone who prefers to go offshore drilling which requires them to spend weeks at a time in different locations away from their family.

It is possible that you know from your own experiences what your wants and needs are. However, if you don't, here is an exercise with a twofold purpose. The first is to discover what some of your main wants and needs are, and the second is to overcome the Those Were the Days syndrome.

Exercise 13—These Can Be the Days

You will need a pen and your journal, or your Word document. It will be helpful to be in a quiet place where you will not be disturbed.

1. **Pick a memory of a time that was so good that you would not mind reliving it. Relax and visualize the memory because this will bring back the feelings in a stronger way than just writing it.**
2. **Answer the following two questions:**

   - **Why was this experience better than what I am experiencing now?**
   - **What wants and needs were being met at that time?**

3. **This is where you will use your imagination. Make a list of ways for you to make sure that those needs will be met.**

4. **Now pick a memory that was not so good. Write why you did not like what was happening.**
5. **Take the memory from Step 4 and visualize it the way you would have liked it to be.**
6. **Write what needs and wants were being met in your visualization in Step 5.**
7. **Brainstorm again as you did in Step 3. What can you do to make sure these needs are met now?**
8. **Make a plan for how you could go about making sure these needs are met now.**

If you were unable to identify your needs, you could look at the memory as something that you used to like doing. For example, you are an unemployed college graduate, but when you were a teenager, you used to go down the shore every weekend when your family owned a house. Obviously you can't afford to buy a million dollar house at the shore. In some places, a million dollars will buy you an acre to pitch your tent. You could plan instead to go down to the shore on weekends with friends for day trips. Perhaps when you have a job again, you could set higher goals and plan to go more often.

Creativity is in order when you are trying to identify ways in which your needs could be met. Keep in mind that there is always more than one way to do anything. Let's imagine that you have a want or a need to be in charge of things. You used to have a job in management, but now instead of being a boss, you have a boss. Maybe outside of work, you can meet your need of being in charge of things by being the president of the local Chamber of Commerce, or perhaps you could organize a food drive. Maybe you could start saving money so that you could start your own business. Be creative!

CHAPTER 14

Your Memories Are Amazing

Throughout this book, you have learned to do all kinds of tricks with your memories. You have learned to retrieve memories and you have learned to eliminate the feelings associated with negative memories. You have also reviewed memories of your past and taken lessons from them. **Imagine if you could learn something from everything that has happened to you, and everything that will happen to you in the future.**

Essentially, this is the ultimate goal of memories. When you can take a lesson from everything that has happened to you, you have mastered your life, and you can be happy about everything that has happened to you. You can look back on your life and see all days as good days.

Healing your memories can make you a happier and more effective person in all areas of life. When you no longer carry the heaviness of all the negative things that may have happened to you, you will begin to see areas in your life changed for the better. The positive effects of healing your memories are also not contained only within the emotional realm. I have seen some of my clients heal themselves emotionally and then also begin to heal themselves physically. Many people who have used the exercises I outlined in this book will tell me that initially, they felt lighter, referring to the removal of an emotional burden, but later, they will contact me to tell me that physical issues have also begun to disappear from their bodies. Many of my clients now feel less stress and have expressed that their days flow more easily after healing their own memories.

Sometimes people who are stuck in the past have trouble setting goals and moving towards the future, but not you! As more memories find their way to the forefront of your mind, you can continue doing the exercises you learned in this book. Additionally, you can access my website www.phenomenalmemory.com or even consider becoming a member of my blog.

Afterword

I hope you have enjoyed reading *Heal Your Memories, Change Your Life*. It can be recourse for you to return to any time for the rest of your life. If you completed the exercises, you know that you can change how you feel about anything and be freed from any negative influences from the past. You can use it on any incident that occurs in the future and treat it as a memory. Even if you do the exercise the next day, it's still a memory.

In my previous books I focused solely on memory improvement. My first book *Living With A Phenomenal Memory* is a memoir. It includes humorous incidents in my life which happened as a result of my memory. Part of the purpose was to send it to universities which were conducting memory studies and offer to be studied. I achieved that purpose when I sent it to the University of California in Irvine where they studied my highly superior autobiographical memory. I and 32 others have been classified.

My second book *Memory Quiz, What Type of Learner Are You?* is available on Kindle. It introduces the idea that you can improve your memory by making connections with facts about your favorite subject and new information. For example, if you are interested in sports and you are studying history, make a connection of a president with a football player. The book can be purchased on my website or on Amazon Kindle.

Having written those two books, I discovered that there are many books on memory improvement and not so many on healing your memories. As a Licensed Professional Counselor and person with highly superior memory, I decided to combine my skills and reach out so that anyone can learn them. It is my wish that you will be free from the past and appreciate everything that you memories have to teach you.

If you feel that you need coaching on memory healing, feel free to visit my website www.phenomenalmemory. com If you become a member you will have access to personal coaching and classes that I will be conducting periodically.

Contributors

I would like to express my deepest thanks to . . . .

My wife Janet, all of your feedback kept me going. It still begins and ends with you. You create many happy memories with me all the time.

Jeanette Baker, thank you for taking my ideas and making them into wonderful illustrations, and illustrating your own ideas. They add spice to the book.

Kate Machugh, thank you for allowing me to share your story. The work that you do to rid the world of bullying is changing the world. Bryant Moore, thank you for sharing your unique perspective. The work that you and Kate do will positively impact society in immeasurable ways.

Kit Summers, thank you for sharing your story. You are an ongoing inspiration that often in life, if plan A falls through try plan B. Nancy Bauser, thank you for sharing your story. No matter what happens and what limitations we have we can strive for more.

Sean Conlon, thank you for being a great friend and having all the unique conversations we have about dates. Keep searching for the right woman.

Dr. Yvonne Kaye, thank you so much for writing the introduction and sharing your story. Years ago you taught me that you can live the life that you want.

About The Author

Frank Healy is a Licensed Professional Counselor in the State of New Jersey and a Certified Life Coach. He is classified as having Highly Superior Autobiographical Memory from the University of California. Frank remembers every day of his life since he was six years old. This includes the day of the week, the weather, news, and personal events. Frank is married and lives in Dennisville, New Jersey. He works as a counselor at AtlantiCare Behavioral Health and Associates for Life Enhancement. Frank's other books include *Living with a Phenomenal Memory* and *Memory Quiz, What Type of Learner are You?*

Frank has been a guest on the Michael Smerkonish Radio Show, and Be The Star You Are. He has been featured on NBC and CBS Health Check in the Philadelphia area. For more information, you can contact Frank through his website, www.phenomenalmemory.com.

Recourses

All In The Family, Stouse, Charles. Adams, Lee "Those Were The Days" www.somglyrics.com

Bauser, Nancy, Disability Life Coach and Trauma Recovery Expert www.survivoracceptance.com Nancy@survivor accdeptance.com

Chopped, www.foodnetwork.com

DSM IV Diagnostic Manual of Mental Disorders

Dyer, Wayne Wishes Fulfilled, 2/2012

Funniest Home Videos www.afu.com

Kaye, Dr. Yvonne. Author of Credit, Cash, and Codependency, and The Child That Never Was. www.yvonnekaye.com

Machugh, Kate. Ugly; The Story of a Bullied Girl www.katemachugh.com

Melonic, Jim

Miller, Dr. Donnel

Moore, Bryant

Robbins, Anthony. Personal Power CD series. 1993 and 1996 Guthy Renker

Summers, Kit. Author of Beyond Your Potential, The Comeback Kit from Coma to Comedy. www.kitsummers.com

"The Times of Your Life" www.lyricsfreak.com

"The Way We Were" www.lyricsfreak.com

"Those Were The Days" www.lyricsmode.com

"Stronger" www.metrolyrics.com

www.ingramcontent.com/pod-product-compliance
Lightning Source LLC
Chambersburg PA
CBHW020412290526
45785CB00002B/519